Roadside

RELIGION

In Search of the Sacred, the Strange, and the Substance of Faith

Timothy K. Beal

BEACON PRESS
BOSTON   01/07   3x

Beacon Press
25 Beacon Street
Boston, Massachusetts 02108-2892
www.beacon.org

Beacon Press books
are published under the auspices of
the Unitarian Universalist Association of Congregations.

08 07 06 05 8 7 6 5 4 3 2 1

This book is printed on acid-free paper that meets the uncoated paper
ANSI/NISO specifications for permanence as revised in 1992.

Text design by Bob Kosturko
Composition by Wilsted & Taylor Publishing Services

Library of Congress Cataloging-in-Publication Data

Beal, Timothy K. (Timothy Kandler), 1963–
Roadside religion : in search of the sacred, the strange,
and the substance of faith / Timothy K. Beal.
p. cm.
ISBN 0-8070-1062-6 (cloth : alk. paper)
1. Christian shrines—United States. 2. Popular culture—United States.
3. United States—Religious life and customs. 4. Christian shrines—Southern States.
5. Popular culture—Southern States. 6. Southern States—Religious life and
customs. 7. Popular culture—Religious aspects—Christianity. I. Title.

BV896.U6B43 2005
203'.5'0973—dc22
2004024185

In memory of my dad, Clay G. Beal
1932–2003

CONTENTS

Introduction

Our twenty-nine-foot rented motor home rested precariously on the shoulder of a county road in the low rolling hills of southern Alabama, just outside the town of Prattville. It was midday mid-June, and the sun was beating down through a cloudless sky. The view from the motor home's "family-room" window: thousands of makeshift wooden crosses leaning this way and that. Some were only a couple feet high, hastily slapped together from scrap wood. Others, towering from a crumbling bluff above the road, were taller than telephone poles. Most of them bore messages, brushed on in red or black or white capital letters:

> YOU WILL DIE
>
> HELL IS HOT HOT HOT

Among the crosses were scrap wood and rusty metal boxes bearing similar proclamations and warnings:

> GOD SAID THE WORLD COMING TOO A END
>
> RICH MAN IN HELL REPENT

In the ditch near our motor home, a rust brown fridge leaned back in the brush as if better to display its message:

> IN HELL FROM SEX SEX

A few yards farther up the road, a makeshift row of old metal housings from air-conditioning window units lined a dirt driveway like junkyard luminarias, each cleverly conveying a message with a refrigeration theme:

NO ICE WATER IN HELL! FIRE HOT!

TOO LATE IN HELL FIRE WATER

These AC luminarias led the way to the tiny ranch-style home of Bill and Marzell Rice, creators and proprietors of this eleven-acre collage of shouting crosses and junked appliances that they call Cross Garden.

My wife, Clover, and our two kids, Sophie, eleven, and Seth, seven, had decided to wait in the motor home while I talked with Bill and Marzell about their unusual horticulture. I had been in the house with them for a couple hours, and as Clover told me later, the

Cross Garden, Prattville, Alabama

motor home's air conditioner, powered by a gas generator, had begun to fail in the midday Alabama heat. The propane-operated fridge wasn't staying cold, and the hot dogs and fruit inside were beginning to compost. What's more, the water supply had run out. That was my fault. In our rush to leave Atlanta that morning, I had neglected to refill the water tank.

Sophie was relaxing on the bed, her belly full of Cocoa Puffs. Clover sat on the couch, trying to avoid the view of Cross Garden, flipping distractedly through the pages of a picture book she'd been reading with Seth. Seth had taken a break from reading to go to the "bathroom," a tiny toileted closet just big enough to sit down, stand up, and turn around in. Forgetting that the water tank was empty, he pressed the "flush" button. Clover heard the sputtering and whirring of the electric pump as it strained to draw the last drops from the tank. Then she heard Seth's bloodcurdling cry, "Help! Mom! It's *spraying* at me!" She looked up from the book and out the window. HELL IS HOT HOT HOT. So it is. And there was my family, parked on the shoulder of what appeared to be one of its innermost circles.

How did we get there?

Although we'd been on the road for less than two weeks at that point, our voyage into the strange and sometimes wonderful religious worlds of roadside America had really begun several months earlier, on another road trip. We were driving from DC to Cleveland through the Appalachian Highlands of northwestern Maryland on Interstate 68. As we crested a rolling hill just outside the quaint old town of Frostburg, we saw what initially looked like a steel girder framework for a four-floor parking garage standing alone in a grassy field about fifty yards from the highway. In front of it was a large blue sign:

NOAH'S ARK BEING REBUILT HERE!

God's Ark of Safety, Frostburg, Maryland

A multilevel parking garage in such a place as this would have been unusual enough. But Noah's Ark? We whizzed past the Ark-in-progress that day, but I knew I'd be back to learn more about this project and its nowaday Noah.

I started keeping a list of roadside religious attractions throughout the country. Soon that list had become an itinerary for a new research project, a roadside approach to discovering religion in America. Six months later, in the summer of 2002, I loaded my family into a rented motor home and hit the rural highways of the Bible Belt on an initial voyage that included visits to places like Golgotha Fun Park, the World's Largest Ten Commandments, Paradise Gardens, Ave Maria Grotto, Holy Land USA and, yes, Cross Garden. Over the next year, I made pilgrimages to many other roadside religious attractions throughout the United States, from the World's Largest Rosary Collection in Skamania County, Washington, to Precious Moments Inspiration Park in Carthage, Missouri, to The Holy Land Experience in Orlando, Florida. I took notes, took pictures, took video, talked with the creators, talked with visitors, talked with Clover and the kids. In the course of these travels in the novel, often strange, sometimes disturbing worlds of roadside religion, I not only discovered new dimensions of the American religious landscape, but I also discovered new religious dimensions of my family and myself. Indeed, what began as a research agenda, albeit a novel one, has become a much more personal, dare I say religious project, as much about my own complex, often ambivalent, relationship to the life of faith as it is about the places and people visited.

Outsider Religion

If you've logged more than a hundred miles of rural American highway in your life, you've probably seen the signs for religious attractions, beckoning you to get off at the next exit and experience whatever it is for yourself: the world's tallest Jesus or teariest Blessed Virgin Mary, replicas of the Wilderness Tabernacle or empty tomb, re-creations of Jerusalem, Rome, paradise, hell. When you drive by such outrageous religious spectacles, your first reaction is likely to be "*What?!?*," blurted out in a burst of laughter. But if you let the place linger in your mind a little longer than it takes to disappear in your rearview mirror, other more interesting questions arise. Questions like "*Who?*" Who did this? Who has the chutzpah in this day and age to do something like *that* on the side of a road? And *why?* What drives such a person? What desires? What visions? What spirits or demons, entrepreneurial and otherwise? In other words, you want to understand. You want to know, *What's the story?*

That's what this book is about. Each chapter focuses on one particular attraction, telling the story of my visit there in words and pictures, reflecting on the meaning of the place as an expression of religious imagination and experience. In each case, I want to discover not only *what* it is, but *who* is behind it and *why* they did it. I want to discover what the story is. Although there's much humor and novelty to enjoy in the stories I tell about these places and the people who create them, I take care to avoid the temptation to make fun or condescend. I want to take these places seriously as unique expressions of religious imagination and unique testimonials to the varieties of religious experience in America.

Granted, this is not the usual approach to studying religion. The usual approach involves delving into a religious tradition's normative scriptures and doctrines, or focusing on established religious institutions and ritual practices. That's not what I'm doing here. On the contrary, I'm focusing on places that most people—religious people and religion scholars alike—would consider *aberrant* forms of religious expression. Although many of these places draw inspiration from the Bible, for example, their uses of it are far from normative or illustrative of the ways biblical interpretation functions within any religious mainstream. Few would consider writing the Ten Commandments in five-foot-tall concrete letters on the side of a mountain, or using miniature golf to tell the story of creation, or fabricating Noah's Ark from steel girders, to be exemplary biblical interpretation. These places are not likely to appear as illustrations in the next edition of Huston Smith's bestselling textbook, *The World's Religions*. And yet, beyond the sheer novelty of such excursions beyond the mainstreams of religious life, I find that these places reveal much about the American religious landscape. Indeed, I believe that religion is often most fascinating, and most revealing, where it's least expected.

In the art world, "outsider art" generally refers to the work of artists without formal training who stand outside the cultural norms of "fine art" schools, museums, and galleries. Bearing little or no relation to trends and developments in contemporary artistic techniques and subjects, outsider art, or *art brut*, was identified by its earliest appreciators especially with children and adults who suffered from mental illnesses that isolated them from mainstream ways of seeing and artistic expression. While the term has expanded to include the works of many who operate outside the formal institutions and values of the professional art world, and while new terms have been coined to indicate important nuances (e.g. "self-taught" and "vernacular"), outsider art continues to be appreciated above all as a form of creativity that finds expression on the social and conceptual fringes of experience.

In a similar sense, I suggest we think of these roadside religious spectacles as works of "outsider religion." Just as the highly individual works of outsider art can often powerfully reveal the breadth and depth of human creativity and imagination in very local, particular forms, so the places explored in this book can reveal the breadth and depth of human religious experience and expression. Paradoxically, it is precisely in their marginality that they open avenues for exploring themes and issues that are central to American religious life, such as pilgrimage, the nostalgia for lost origins, the desire to recreate sacred time and space, creativity as religious devotion, apocalypticism, spectacle, exile, and the relation between religious vision and social marginality. So "outsider religion" becomes a way of illuminating "insider religion."

Making Space

In many respects, the places we visit in this book are as unique as the individuals who have created them. Yet I do believe that there are certain family resemblances among them. Above all, each is fundamentally about *creating sacred space*.

What do I mean by that? In particular, what do I mean by "sacred"? Drawn from the Latin *sacer*, the most basic meaning of "sacred" is "set apart." But what sets it apart as such? Different theorists of religion give very different answers. For Émile Durkheim, the answer was sociological: the sacred is that which symbolizes and indeed creates the social and moral coherence of the community. It is, in other words, that which a social group (a clan, a church) sets apart to represent and create unity. For others, the answer is phenomenological, that is, it's a matter of understanding how the sacred is perceived and experienced as such. French philosopher Georges Bataille, for example, described the sacred as that which is experienced as radical otherness, representing a realm (real or imaginary) of animal intimacy that threatens to annihilate the social and symbolic order in a holy conflagration; as such it is both alluring and terrifying, and religion's job is to mediate between it and the established order of things. For historian of religion Mircea Eliade, too, the sacred is wholly other, but he focuses on the religious person's experience of it as an experience of transcendence that serves to orient her within a sacred cosmic order.

In the context of this book, we focus on the sacred primarily in the phenomenological sense, as that which is set apart on account of its relation to the transcendent—that is, in most cases we encounter here, God. So, when I say that each of the places we explore in this book is fundamentally about creating sacred space, I mean that each works to create a space that is set apart in a way that orients it toward and opens it to divine transcendence. Founded on, inspired by, and organized around deeply personal religious experiences, each of these places is a very concrete manifestation of the desire to create a place that is set apart from ordinary space, from the homogeneity of everyday life, an otherworldly realm governed by rules "other" than those of normal profane space.

The means by which spaces are set apart as sacred vary. Many use boundaries such as walls or wooded areas that give a sense of enclosure, cutting our senses off from the sights and sounds of the world outside. Some play with size, creating miniatures or enlargements that defy perceptual and conceptual normality, giving us the feeling that we are in an "other" fantasy world or dream space in which normal scales don't apply. Similarly, some use *artificial nature*, creating flowers, plants, and animals out of concrete, metal, marbles, and other cultural discards. Blurring the line between nature and artifice, these elements add to the sense of otherworldliness. Some employ what we might call "religious re-creation," making miniature or full-size replicas of sacred spaces from other parts of the world (the Jerusalem Temple, the Wilderness Tabernacle, the Dome of the Rock, St. Peter's Basilica) or from the mythological worlds of ancient scriptures (Noah's Ark, the Tower of Babel). Some of these go so far as to create whole microcosms of well-known sacred spaces (Rome, Jerusalem, or the entire "land of the Bible"). Some employ all of these strategies. In any case, the aim—which may be more or less conscious—is to set the space apart from its surroundings, making it a holy world unto itself, governed by its own rules, which are "other" than those of profane space.

As creations of sacred space, the roadside religious spectacles we explore in this book are in some respects not so different from the more mainstream, "insider" religious spaces of temples, churches, mosques, synagogues, memorials, and monasteries. They too work to create an experience of being set apart, in another world. They too are usually founded on, inspired by, and organized around some revelation or similar original religious experience—a miracle, a vision, or the giving of a new law, for example. And they too are created to host the religious experiences of those who enter, individually and collectively. The differences come into play with regard to the symbolic meanings of the elements themselves. In insider religious spaces, such meanings are held in common, taken for granted as part of a shared communal repertoire of words and images and spatial boundaries. There, the sacred is the social, in the Durkheimian sense we discussed earlier. In the outsider religious spaces we explore here, on the other hand, such meanings are more personal, located in the particular and peculiar experiences and beliefs and practices of the individual responsible for each place. Although we are welcomed into that space, hosted by it, and although we are aware that the space is in some sense a form of expression and communication, its content, its meaning, remains in very profound ways ultimately inaccessible, strange, foreign. This is so even when the space itself is located within the context of a larger public religious space, as we will see with Ave Maria Grotto, a microcosm of miniature buildings and shrines created by Brother Joseph Zoettl on the campus of St. Bernard Abbey in Cullman, Alabama. Set in the context of an institutional Catholic community of worship and education, it is nonetheless a world unto itself, a uniquely personal space of divine revelation.

Indeed, these places reflect deep tensions between, on the one hand, the highly personal, even private experiences and meanings of their creators, and, on the other hand, the desire to share those experiences in a very public way. Each is a very outward, public expression of a very inward, private religious life. Each is a creative public response to a profoundly life-changing personal experience. There's something about that experience that won't let go, that insists on being communicated, translated to others in spectacular form. In some cases, as we'll see, the process of "going public" that results in such roadside religious attractions can be very painful. As such, they are difficult to make sense of according to Durkheim's theory of the sacred as the social. On the one hand, they are highly individual and particular. They are expressions of personality and, in some sense, untranslatable experience. On the other hand, they are highly social. They are gestures of invitation and forms of communication to others. Indeed, in some cases, such as Howard Finster's Paradise Gardens, they beget new forms of religious community.

These places are as deeply personal as they are public. At the creative heart and soul of each is a religious imagination trying to give outward form to inner experience. It's no coincidence that most of these roadside religious spectacles are also private homes. In one sense, this is simply a practical matter: one starts where one is, and most of these people aren't rich or fundraising-savvy enough even to consider other locations. But I think there's more to it than that. What is home, after all? An extension of myself, a shelter from the storm, a piece of private property, a locus of intimacy and secrets. But also a public expression of myself, reflecting on me and my family, a place of hospitality, of welcoming strangers, an address where people can find me. Home is, paradoxically, both private and public, individual and social. So too the roadside religious attractions we visit in this book.

It is above all this outrageous gesture of self-exposure, this desire to communicate a very personal, perhaps incommunicable religious experience in such a public, even spectacular way that I find so personally disarming. It's an invitation to relationship, with me or anyone who visits. That I didn't anticipate, and that has made all the difference.

Strange Familiar

My daughter, Sophie, recently told me what she thinks of my work as a religion scholar. She said it seems that what I like to do is make creepy things interesting. One of my university colleagues suggests that maybe she means the reverse, that is, I like to make interesting things creepy. Either way, I like it. In fact, I tell my students that the study of religion is fundamentally about *making the strange familiar and the familiar strange.* It's about encountering religious ideas, practices, traditions, and institutions that initially appear to us as "other," disturbingly foreign, and coming to a point where we understand how they can make sense given a certain set of circumstances. Such work requires not only critical rigor and tenacity in order to elaborate those circumstances; it also requires imagination in order to put oneself in another's situation. Indeed, understanding is always in some sense about coming to see how something could make sense, could be true and meaningful, within a certain context, according to certain conditions, according to a certain story.

And getting to know another's story is perhaps the best place to start. We humans are shaped by narrative. We live story-shaped lives in a story-shaped world. Our stories tell us who we are, where we are, and when we are. We construe ourselves and our lives in story form. We tell stories to make meaning out of our lives, to locate ourselves within a larger narrative horizon. And by our own narrative imaginations we are able to enter into the story worlds of others. Not that we occupy those story worlds in the same way they do. But in sharing stories, we share the spaces in which we make meaning in terms of where we've been, where we are, and where we're going.

We might think of understanding, then, as an act of narrative imagination. It's about trying to bridge otherness by finding my way into the other's story. But I can never understand completely. I can never become the other I wish to understand. To presume I can is dangerous, because then I risk reducing the other, incommensurably rich in particularity, complexity, and wonderful strangeness, to myself. And that is a form of violence. It kills the face of the other.

Yet in my effort to imagine otherness, to let the other into myself, to understand, I end up becoming *other to myself*. I become less comfortable in my own skin. My own familiar begins to seem strange. I become a stranger to myself. Which is why I say that the study of religion is about making the strange familiar *and* making the familiar strange. In the effort to make the strange familiar, the familiar becomes less familiar.

I experienced this dynamic of religious understanding on many occasions in the course of my travels. Our family visit to Cross Garden is a good example. As I climbed out of the motor home and wandered around that eleven-acre collage of fire-and-brimstone-preaching crosses and apocalyptic appliances, my initial experience was an irreducible mix of amusement and monumental horror. On the one hand, focusing on the crudely made individual pieces with their often ironic messages, I wanted to laugh out loud. On the other hand, enveloped in the total world that these individual pieces come together to create, I felt an overwhelming desire to climb into the motor home's captain chair and get the hell out of there. In both senses, in relation to the individual objects and in relation to the total experience of the place, Cross Garden was other, foreign, profoundly strange. But as I talked with Bill and Marzell Rice and got to know their story, my feeling about the place, and them, began to change. I began to feel at home in their world. I came to recognize this place as an expression of profound religious experience. Not that I identified with their experience completely, but I could hear the story, get into it, see how it could be true, and from within that story, see Cross Garden as a genuine expression of it. For them, as we'll see, it's not a scary place but a safe place, a nest, an ark in the storm. So as Bill and Marzell welcomed me into their family room and their family story, the strangeness of Cross Garden became less strange.

By the end of our conversation, Bill was asking me about my own family and our story. He loved children, and when he learned that Clover and the kids were waiting for me in the motor home across the road, he begged me to invite them over. I trotted across the cross-strewn yard and over to the motor home to fetch them. "Bill wants to meet you," I said as I peeked in through the screen door. "What do you say?"

The kids glanced anxiously at each other, then at me and Clover, then out the window, then back at each other, red-faced and sweaty from being holed up in the motor home for hours. "Really? Do we have to?"

As we walked across the road, past the high bluff of crosses ("You will die."), up the AC-housing-lined driveway ("No ice water in Hell. Fire hot!"), and into the front yard, Bill rolled out in his electric scooter chair to greet us, Marzell close behind. Smiles beamed from their faces. As Clover and the kids warmly but (I could see) anxiously approached to shake Bill's hand, I began to realize that in the process of making the Rice family's strangeness more familiar to me, I had become a little strange in relation to my own familiars. I found myself somewhere between Bill and Marzell on the one hand and my own family on the other. And I found myself in the role of mediator, but with no idea how to mediate other than to tell the whole story as they had told it to me. I did so later, but at that moment it was impossible.

This, then, is a book about the strange familiar, and the familiar strange. And what more remarkable combinations of the strange and the familiar could there be than such roadside religious attractions? Surely there's nothing more familiar to the American land-scape than highways and religion. And nothing could be stranger than a roadside attraction like Cross Garden or a life-size Noah's Ark in progress. What better places, then, to discover the familiar in the strange, and vice versa?

The Roman playwright Terence famously declared, "I am human, so nothing human is alien to me." Most of us claim to believe this. I think most of us really want to believe it. But perhaps we're also a lit-tle uneasy about testing it too hard. Perhaps that's what keeps most of us away from the places that are the subject of this book. Indeed, for as long as I can remember, I've been speeding by, fascinated if also wary, resisting their strange attraction, renouncing them in devo-tion to my destination. But now I'm watching for the signs, taking the exits, hoping to find out what the story is, and in the process to make it part of my own story.

Home-a-Roam

In our little suburban town of Shaker Heights, Ohio, where by fourth or fifth grade many kids are beginning to think seriously about where they want to go to college, lots of families take summer road trips with educational themes. They follow the route of Lewis and Clark or the Trail of Tears. They explore Yosemite or the Grand Canyon. They visit famous battlefields or colonial settlements. They tour great art museums or attend Shakespeare festivals. So, Clover and I thought, why not make this initial exploration of roadside reli-gion into our own little family travel seminar? Not that it would help the kids get into accelerated classes or improve their proficiency scores. But it would be an opportunity for them to encounter, dis-cuss, and try to understand expressions of religious experience and imagination quite unfamiliar to them. And they were sure to enrich our little seminar with perspectives very different from my own or Clover's.

I should mention that Clover is an ordained Presbyterian minister. With a minister and a religion professor for parents, our kids stood little chance of getting out of this one.

Many of the places on our itinerary for this inaugural excursion, which concentrated on the Bible Belt, were well off the beaten path and far from the off-ramp clusters of Super 8s, HoJos, and Red Roof Inns. Lodging might be hard to find, we thought. So we decided to make our ride our home, that is, to rent a motor home.

The idea of making this trip in a motor home immediately appealed to the kids. A motor home seemed to them like utopia on wheels. Ms. Frizzle's Magic School Bus paled by comparison. They stared wide-eyed at pictures of the floor plans provided by rental companies. You mean there are beds for each of us in the back? And there's a couch and two chairs and a table for playing games? And a TV? And a kitchen with a microwave? And cupboards for chips and a fridge for pop?

The kids were sold. I wager we could have proposed a tour of Arkansas's largest chicken slaughterhouses and they would have eagerly agreed to it, so long as they could log all the miles while sitting on a sofa eating sugary cereal and watching videos or lying in the twin beds in the back bedroom playing cards.

We rented our motor home from Tonie's RV in Salem, Virginia, just outside Roanoke. Tonie was a warm and sprightly sixtysomething woman with an obvious head for business and a love for RVing and RVers. Her operation consisted of a parts store and a large hanger-like garage located at the end of a narrow road next to the railroad tracks. Tonie ran the repair shop, sold parts, and rented out several older-model motor homes and conversion vans.

Tonie clearly took great pride in her small fleet. (Let me stress that it was my fault, not hers, that we ran out of water in Alabama. And it was also my fault that the fridge thawed out. She admonished me to check its pilot light whenever we were parked at a tilt.) Her favorite motor home was one she called *Cream Puff*, a 1980s Jamboree that she claimed rode better than any of the newer fancy tanks on the road these days. But *Cream Puff* didn't have enough sleeping space for our family, so she set us up with her next favorite, a twenty-nine-foot Coachmen that she had acquired several years earlier from an older couple down in Florida. It had been their pride and joy, and they had given it many personal touches, including curtains, special floormats, and hand-made wooden holders for paper towels, mugs, and dish sponges. It had a queen bed above the cab, a little living room with a sofa and two chairs, a kitchenette, a bathroomette, a showerette, and two twin beds in a back bedroom. It was the perfect mobile home for our foursome.

As anyone can see from a quick scan of the spare tire covers and license plates on the motor homes in Tonie's parking lot, there's something about the open road that makes you want to name your ride. Maybe it's because your vehicle is in some sense an extension of yourself, like a turtle's shell. Or maybe it's a way of christening your ride as a travel companion. Aware that his friends reckoned as foolishness his 1960 cross-country road trip with his dog, Charley, John Steinbeck named his specially designed camper truck *Rocinante*, after Don Quixote's beloved steed, which translates roughly as "superlative nag," or maybe "supreme packhorse." It had a V-6 engine, an automatic transmission, and an extra-large generator. Steinbeck painted the name in a bold Spanish-looking script on the passenger-side door. It was, in quixotic Steinbeck's adoring eyes, "a beautiful thing, powerful and lithe," and rarely let him down.

In his 1978 search for authenticity along the old two-lane "blue highways" of America, William Least Heat-Moon named his ride *Ghost Dancing*. This "wheel estate," as his mechanic called it, was a Ford Econoline van fitted with all the accoutrements necessary to convert it from "a clangy tin box into a place at once a six-by-ten bedroom, kitchen, bathroom, parlor." The name *Ghost Dancing*, Heat-Moon admits, was "a heavy-handed symbol" referring to the "desperate resurrection rituals" of the Plains Indians in the 1890s, calling for "the return of warriors, bison, and the fervor of the old life that would sweep away the new." Having left his job and his wife, his departure in *Ghost Dancing* was a similarly desperate resurrection dance, a romantic quest for connection and a rebirth of wonder: "With a nearly desperate sense of isolation and a growing suspicion that I lived in an alien land, I took to the open road in search of places where change did not mean ruin and where time and men and deeds connected." Referring back to the desperate dances that were the death throws of an ancient dream of rebirth, the van's name gave expression to Heat-Moon's own nostalgia for lost origins and hope for resurrection.

The name we gave our "wheel estate" reflected no kindred sense of disconnection or alienation, no longing to escape relationships or fates. We took home with us intact. The name came to us by accident but immediately captured our familial sense of adventure. Clover and I were on a springtime stroll through our neighborhood, and Seth was toodling down the sidewalk ahead of us on his BMX bike. "Dad," he called back over his shoulder, "when are we leaving in the... What's it called? Home-a-roam?" Perfect. It rolled off the tongue nicely and had the same number of syllables as "motor home," but with a twist that captured Seth's—and our—sense of what this trip was about. The miracle of this vehicle wasn't that it was a motorized home but that it was a roaming home. It gave us the power to take up our home and roam.

So began my "blue highways" approach to discovering religion in America, as a family adventure and multigenerational travel seminar. On that first trip, we logged about 4,000 miles in a little less than a month, covering nine states and visiting a dozen sites along the way. Our route formed a figure eight: Ohio to Virginia (where we rented the motor home) to North Carolina to Georgia to Alabama to Tennessee to Kentucky to West Virginia to Virginia (where we returned the motor home) to Maryland to Ohio. Many of the chapters in this book focus on places we visited on that initial trip. Others focus on places I've visited on subsequent excursions throughout the United States—some with family (all or part) in tow, some by myself, but never again, sadly, in our *Home-a-Roam*.

Divine Madness

This is a book *about* religion. But in another sense, I must confess, it's also a *religious* book.

Every road trip carries with it the possibility of renewal. As you break from the familiar commute and journey into the *terra incognita*, that "unknown territory" where be monsters, and angels, and where it's sometimes hard to tell which is which, you open yourself to receiving an unexpected blessing, a moment of revelation that might bring new life. Perhaps you take to the road with the explicit aim of wresting such a blessing by discovering the world beyond your world. But what you end up discovering may be something more profoundly transformative and re-creative: yourself beyond yourself, in other words, self-transcendence.

What desire for renewal or transcendence, what resurrection hope, what spirit has driven me into the religious *terra incognita* of roadside America? I don't think I could have answered that question when I began this project. But as I look back now, I can see that I've been motivated by something more than my admitted fascination with religious kitsch, and something more than my intellectual interest in making sense of these places as expressions of lived religion worth our attention. On a more personal level, I've been driven by a desire to venture beyond the secure borders of my own self-assured cynicism in order to encounter faith in all its awesome absurdity.

Faith, as the New Testament letter to the Hebrews puts it, is "the substance of things hoped for, the evidence of things not seen." It is the religious antithesis of cynicism, which, for all its clever love of irony and detached social commentary, is also a form of self-protection against risking belief in anything uncertain. Faith is about devoting oneself, body and mind, to that which is not evidently there, visible, verifiable, but in which one hopes and believes without the possibility of certainty. It's a divine madness whose hope comes, as philosopher Søren Kierkegaard famously put it, "by virtue of the absurd." Kierkegaard was endlessly fascinated by the madness of Abraham, absurdly faithful to God's command even to the point of sacrificing his beloved son. There's something likewise endlessly fascinating to me about the madness of someone who is compelled to spend a lifetime giving form to his vision of a life-size Noah's Ark on a mountaintop, or re-creating the Holy Land in the Blue Ridge Mountains. In the eyes of the world, these are indeed works of faith whose only virtue is absurdity. But by the same token I find them utterly, disarmingly sincere, without the slightest hint of irony. No knowing winks, no tongues in cheeks. And so I find myself compelled to peek over the fences of cynicism and ironic detachment, fences that too often enclose my daily commute through this world, in hopes of catching a glimpse of something of the substance of faith.

Not that I'm entirely removed from the life of faith. I'm no pure cynic when it comes to religion. But my relationship to my own religious tradition is as tentative and complicated as it is abiding and deep.

I was raised in two worlds that appear to most to be mutually excusive. The first is that white suburban American world of Generation X, baptized in a shared popular media culture and characterized above all by a general skepticism regarding the value of working within established systems, political and religious alike, as well as by a general feeling of powerlessness to find other ways of working for change in the world.

But I also grew up with a clear religious identity within a particular religious culture, namely conservative evangelicalism. And that has made all the difference. While steeped in the general Gen X pop culture—Sex Pistols and Talking Heads, Watergate and the Cold War, *Gilligan's Island* and *Love Boat*, Pop Rocks and Maui Wowie— my childhood and teen years were also pervaded by family prayers before meals (even in restaurants, much to my sister's and my embarrassment), Vacation Bible School (at age six I won a prize for being the first in my VBS class to memorize all the books of the Old Testament), Friday night hymn sings around the piano, high school youth groups (my parents were Young Life leaders), mission trips, the Four Spiritual Laws, and that brown spiral songbook with the fish on the cover (you either know what I mean or you don't).

Yet there is considerable distance between me and that particular form of Christianity now. I no longer would call myself a conservative evangelical—nor would anyone else call me either or both of those terms. And I'm sure many conservative evangelicals would hesitate to call me a Christian at all. Following a well-worn and well-documented path of spiritual development among my peers, I grew alienated from that culture and its theology during college.

That's not to say that I have rejected Christianity or the church altogether, however. Although I can atheist anyone under the table on some days, I remain a Christian, and I remain committed to the church, albeit a far more progressive, socially and politically radical vision of the church than the one I grew up with, a church that sees the work of the Gospel as the very this-worldly work of liberation and reconciliation, of sanctifying life, of letting suffering speak, and of letting justice roll down like waters. I am a member of a local church, and I go with my family nearly every Sunday. Clover is one of the ministers (which I suppose makes me a minister's wife), and I sincerely believe in her calling to that ministry. Moreover, I myself teach Sunday school there. But the way I teach it is a far cry from the way it was taught when I was a kid. My aim above all is to create a space for us to ask questions, ultimate questions, the kind that survive all the answers given them. Preferring Cicero's alternative etymology of religion—not *religare*, "rebind," but *relegere*, "reread"—I see it less as a binding system of beliefs or set of doctrines and more as a process of rereading, reexamining, reinterpreting inherited traditions. For me, the religious life is a communal practice of reading again, of opening the book and cracking its binding, of raising new questions and creating new meanings in new contexts. My favorite biblical books are the ones that do just that—reread and question inherited tradition—within the canon of scripture: Job, in which the model of faith is a man whose abject suffering makes him desperate and disoriented enough to challenge God and the moral order of God's creation as attested in the Torah; Ecclesiastes, in which a sage wonders whether all that passes as wisdom is nothing but vapor; and Esther, which imagines a world much like ours in which politics are driven by insecurity and in which God appears to be altogether absent. Above all I want to attend to those places in biblical literature, in Christian tradition, and in the life of faith in which our established discourse—our theological answering machine—breaks down, cracks open, and points beyond itself to a wholly other mystery that cannot be captured or represented.

Yet another level of complexity in my religious life grows out of my work as a professor and researcher in the academic study of religion—a profession, by the way, in which you'll find a great many ex-evangelicals, along with countless other lapsed or disaffected religious types. Studying various beliefs, practices, and institutions of religions (including my own) from historical and crosscultural perspectives, as social and psychological phenomena, creates within me a certain distance from my own religious life. I often find myself treating my own religious practices and beliefs as data along with those drawn from other sources. Doing so creates an experience of self-objectification, something like a lucid dream. And dreaming when you know you're dreaming is something very different from just dreaming.

No doubt rereading Christian tradition as I try to do in the church and studying it from academic perspectives as I try to do in the university are my ways of negotiating and making sense of my own inheritance from conservative evangelical Christianity without abandoning the religious life altogether. No doubt.

Some would say that religion is like a raft. For a religion to be worth its salt, it has to be seaworthy enough to carry you across life's deepest, stormiest, most chaotic waters. And a raft of questions, riddled with theological leaks and tears, won't carry you very far. Perhaps that's my religion, and I won't realize it till I'm in over my head. Or perhaps I feel so securely buoyed by the faith of my childhood, the faith of my fathers, the faith of my minister wife, that I'm not afraid to peek over the sides of the raft into the abyss. And perhaps that's a kind of faith, albeit a borrowed one.

But it's not the kind of faith that Kierkegaard is talking about. It's not the kind of faith that hears God talking. It's not the kind of faith that leads you to take your son on a walk up Mount Moriah, or build an ark on a mountaintop in Maryland, or plant a garden of crosses on a country road in Alabama.

Not that I want that kind of faith. I don't think I do. But I find it strangely compelling in its exuberance, its willingness to risk all, its divine madness.

Chapter One

BIBLICAL RECREATION

Holy Land USA
Bedford County, Virginia

My family and I were sitting toward the back of the second of two flatbed trailers that were hitched together and snaking along a winding dirt road behind an old boxy four-wheel-drive pickup. The trailer-truck combination had been converted from something distinctly farmy to a relatively comfortable open-air touring train. Each of the flatbeds was covered by a corrugated metal roof and had two rows of padded school bus seats bolted to its wooden floor.

We were coming to the end of Journey Trail, the three-mile loop road through the foothills of Virginia's Blue Ridge Mountains that takes visitors to the various exhibits of Holy Land USA, a roughly 1:100 scale replication of the land of the Bible during the time of Jesus. This not-for-profit, nondenominational ministry runs solely on donations, hosting more than twenty-five thousand visitors per year—as many as five hundred on a Saturday during peak season. Most come in church groups from Virginia or North Carolina. We were sharing our tour along Journey Trail with a group from an African-American church in North Carolina—forty women plus the bus driver and two husbands.

Our truck driver, Mike, was also our tour guide. An energetic, warm-hearted, forty-something family man, he lives and works on the property of Holy Land USA along with his wife, eight daughters, and five sons. He keeps the animals, repairs the trucks, maintains the trails, and gives guided tours.

At key points along the way, Mike would stop the truck, hop out, strap on his portable sound system (a small amplifier and handheld mike that reminded me of one of those Mr. Microphones from the 1970s), and give us a minilecture on our current virtual location, be it the stable where Jesus was born, Joseph's woodworking shop, or the Dome of the Rock.

As we lurched to a stop along the dirt road near an old wooden building labeled "Upper Room," a woman seated in the row ahead of us called out, "Where *are* we?" She and her fellow traveler had been talking about their church group's long bus ride that morning, during which they had lost track of how far they'd come.

I was about to answer that we were in Bedford County, Virginia, when our tour guide climbed onto the flatbed and declared in a booming voice, "Jerusalem!"

"What did he say?" the woman asked her friend, scowling in confusion.

Another woman a few rows ahead looked back over her shoulder and repeated with a smile, "Jerusalem. He said we're in Jerusalem."

"Amen." Several other women nodded. "That's right. We're in Jerusalem now!"

Re-creating the Sacred

There is a deep desire within many of us to inhabit our sacred stories, to re-create sacred space and time in the here and now and to live into it with all our heart, mind, and strength. We want to make sacred space and time present. This desire to re-create the sacred— let's call it religious recreation—is a kind of *nostalgia*, homesickness (from ancient Greek *nostos*, "returning home," plus *algia*, "pain"), a longing to have our everyday lives set within the horizon of a sacred story. And in the process to re-create and reconsecrate ourselves and our contemporary world, in which it feels as though our sense of connection with the sacred is always being worn away by the pressures of everyday life. In this respect, religious recreation is something more than our word "recreation" has come to mean. Religious recreation is both the re-creation of the sacred past in the present and the re-creation of the self as sacred. In re-creating time and space as sacred, we re-create ourselves as sacred.

We can see this desire for religious recreation expressed in many ways within traditional Jewish and Christian religion. Local Jewish temples and synagogues, for example, replicate architectural features of the Jerusalem Temple, believed to be founded by God upon the foundation stone of the cosmos; and the makeshift booths built during Succoth replicate the temporary dwellings in which the Israelites lived while wandering in the wilderness. Likewise, Communion tables in Christian churches replicate the table of the Last Supper, Jesus's final communal meal with his disciples.

We see this same kind of nostalgic desire to re-create sacred time and space in the various works of what I call *biblical recreation*: scale re-creations of the land of the Bible, or Jerusalem; life-size re-creations of Noah's Ark or the Wilderness Tabernacle; and so on. Indeed, as historian and biblical scholar Burke O. Long shows in his remarkable *Imagining the Holy Land*, the practices of religious devotion to the Holy Land have deep historical roots in America, going back at least as far as the late nineteenth century. During that time, the combination of new archeological research in Palestine and the rise in popularity of travel narratives and picture books from the Middle East led to an explosion of public interest in the land of the Bible. What emerged was a form of religious devotion that Long, borrowing John Kirtland Wright's term, calls *geopiety*, a deep religious devotion to a vision of the Holy Land concocted from a "curious mix of romantic imagination, historical rectitude, and attachment to physical space." As Long takes pains to make clear, this "land of the Bible" that is the object of such geopietistic devotion is not an actual physical place, past or present. Rather it is a conceptual space, a product of religious devotion and imagination. It is the story world of the Bible placed like a template on the land of Palestine and Israel.

Since the late nineteenth century, American geopiety has found expression not only in popular books tracing the footsteps of Jesus but also in *biblical recreations*, life-size and scaled-down material reconstructions of places and sacred sites from the land of the Bible. One of the most well-known early examples is Palestine Park in Chautauqua, New York, which once included a life-size Tabernacle built to the specifications given in Exodus, a pyramid, a model of Jerusalem, and a small scale replica of the biblical Holy Land itself —complete with a ten-foot-long Dead Sea, a smaller Sea of Galilee, and markers for important biblical sites—landscaped into the rocky terrain of the shoreline of Lake Erie, which serves as the Mediterranean Sea. (Today, about all that remains of Palestine Park is the lakeside replica.) This American geopiety reached a turn-of-the-century entrepreneurial, evangelical, and patriotic peak with the Jerusalem exhibit at the St. Louis World's Fair, which included an elaborate golden Tabernacle, the Dome of the Rock, and live performances.

Holy Land USA is very much part of this American tradition of geopietistic, imaginative practice of re-creating the land of the Bible —albeit in a far more homegrown form than either Chautauqua or the World's Fair.

Like its historical predecessors, Holy Land USA has both private and public dimensions. On the one hand, this two-hundred-and-fifty-acre biblical recreation is an expression of the personal religious desire of its founder, Bob Johnson, to re-create the sacred time and space of the biblical world. On the other hand, it is a venue for others to share that desire with him. A native of the nearby town of Bedford, Mr. Johnson and his son, Campbell, bought the property in 1972 after he retired from his general mercantile business in town. Campbell, who was in poor health and died soon after they closed the purchase, had wanted to preserve the land as a nature sanctuary, whereas Bob wanted to use it to create what he called a "biblical representation," that is, a scale replica of the land of the Bible during the time of Jesus. Thus the subtitle of Holy Land USA on the sign at the main entrance, "A Nature Sanctuary," which bears the desires of both father and son.

By all accounts a very sociable, funny, and generous spirit, Mr. Johnson had a deep and abiding fascination with the land of the Bible and spent the last two-and-a-half decades of his life creating this biblical representation. He made numerous trips to various sites of biblical significance in Israel, each time returning to build new displays on his property, Bible in one hand and tape measure in the other. Thus Holy Land USA is very much a material expression of his own deep desire to imagine and occupy the sacred time and space of the Bible.

On the other hand, Mr. Johnson was clearly motivated by a very public aim to host the same kind of religious desires in others, to provide a context for guests to take a leap of imagination and faith into the footsteps of Jesus. Indeed, he understood his work primarily as a ministry to the people of Bedford. Because most of them would never have the wherewithal to travel to the Holy Land themselves, he said, he wished to bring the Holy Land to them.

Mr. Johnson's desire to host such a religious experience in others was contagious, as is evident from our tour guide Mike's story of his own calling to work there. Indeed, as he shared it with me, his is a call story worthy of the Gospels. He and his family had just moved into the Bedford area from Florida. Mr. Johnson, then in his eighties, knew everyone in town, and when he saw them enter the Golden Corral buffet one evening, he immediately recognized them as new-comers. He rose from his table, called them over from the other side of the room, and invited them to join him for dinner. By dessert, he had convinced them to move into a house on the Holy Land USA property and begin work within two weeks. Mike had been working there ever since, along with several other families who have contin-ued the ministry since Mr. Johnson's death in 1999.

Story World

It is important to understand that Holy Land USA is not simply a re-creation of the land of Israel and Palestine, past or present. Rather, it is a material re-creation of the Gospel story drawn selectively from the Protestant Christian Bible. It is a *story world*, a narrative space. In it biblical narrative is given material form. Its geography is story-shaped, following the life of Jesus from the stable to the tomb, and beyond. The only road through this space, called Journey Trail, takes visitors on a one-way trip through the Gospel narrative: beginning in the south, in Bethlehem, where Jesus was born; then heading north to the Galilee region, where Jesus grew up and began his min-istry; and then turning south and running down the west side of the Jordan river to Jerusalem, arriving finally at Calvary and the empty tomb.

Along Journey Trail there are a dozen or so exhibits, each repre-senting the place of a particular biblical story. We might think of them as stages. But instead of live actors we find two-dimensional figures of biblical characters, cut with a jigsaw from plywood and then painted with bright, contrasting colors. Jesus and Mary both sport halos.

What these figures lack in lifelikeness is more than made up for, it seems to me, in homemade authenticity, earnestness, and a kind of visual allure that's hard to put a finger on. Indeed, they reflect no intention to create realistic images of human beings. The eye-drawing power of these flat, two-dimensional, slightly out-of-proportion figures is more like that of traditional Christian icons. Staring past or through us, their hearts and minds appear to be elsewhere. They seem to be gazing through the world, their eyes fixed on a world beyond this one. As such they invite contemplation of the otherworldly.

Our first stop on the tour was a shepherd's cave built into a dirt mound. In the opening of the cave are several cutout figures: two sheep, a shepherd, an angel, and Joseph. This is a representation of the Gospel scene in which the angel Gabriel tells Joseph what's going on with Mary ("Do not be afraid to take Mary as your wife, for the child conceived in her is from the Holy Spirit. She will bear a son, and you are to name him Jesus, for he will save his people from their sins."). Mike pointed out that this cave construction is closer to the kind of stable in which Jesus was born than the typical small wooden shed one finds in most nativity scenes. As he talked to us, a couple of freshly shorn, real live sheep approached him expectantly, and he fed them a handful of something. Like any good shepherd, Mike knew them by name.

As we continued north on the Jericho Road leg of Journey Trail, along the Jordan River valley, Mike added a little drama to the experience. Reminding us of the Good Samaritan story, he pointed out that such roads in ancient times were prime locations for robbers, who would ambush vulnerable travelers. "But I don't think we need to worry today. No one would dare come after a tough-looking bunch like ours!" Everyone chuckled along with him, clearly enjoying the ride and happy to participate in the virtual experience.

A hundred yards or so beyond the shepherd's cave stands a strange contraption composed of old metal wagon wheels, saw blades, plowshares, gears, a milk can, and sundry other farm antiques. About ten feet tall, it looks like a cross between an old tractor and a very dangerous piece of playground equipment. On it is a sign that reads HEROD'S IDOL, along with Bible verses warning against idolatry and covetousness. This odd piece, Mike explained, is Mr. Johnson's rather fanciful representation of King Herod's hunger for power and his fear of the baby Jesus, whom he learned about from the three wise men. Behind it is an armored figure in a chariot pointed back down Journey Trail toward the shepherd's cave, from whence we had come. With a slight stretch of imagination, it's a centurion off to fulfill Herod's desperate order to slaughter all children under two in and around Bethlehem. On the ground nearby were several old millstones, references to Jesus saying that it would be better for a man to be tossed into the sea with a millstone tied around his neck than for him to offend a child.

At the northernmost point along Journey Trail is a collection of buildings set around a miniature Sea of Galilee, representing the region of ancient Palestine in which Jesus was raised and began his ministry. Encircled by a narrow gravel road, the glassy-surfaced sea is a disturbingly Day-Glo blue-green. The sign on its southernmost shore pleads, WILL YOU HELP US SAVE THE SEA? This is not a biblical reference. Since the county ran a new power line along a nearby ridge a few years ago, the sea has been in ecological crisis. Its water levels are dropping and its algae levels are rising. Unable to influence the local powers that be, Holy Land USA has launched a "Save the Sea" campaign to raise money to clean the pond and restore it to its original holiness.

Just south of the Sea of Galilee there is a smaller pond and a rocky trail leading up to a substantial stone-walled building with a log roof. This is the carpentry workshop of Joseph and Jesus. Inside, standing at a long rustic wooden slab table and surrounded by antique plows, saws, and other old farm equipment are Joseph and a preteen Jesus. Off to the side, in the background, Mary watches father and son adoringly, no doubt pondering it all in her heart.

Anticipating the question on all our minds, Mike hastened to explain all the farm equipment. Socioeconomic life in most of Palestine during the time of Jesus was primarily rural and agricultural. Although different from the tools used way back then, the preindustrial farm equipment interspersed throughout Holy Land USA is meant to remind people of the historical distance between modern American society and that first-century world. I suspect that for many visitors, consciously or not, it also evokes a certain distinctly American nostalgia for this nation's own mythic beginnings of life on the frontier.

On the north end of the sea, close to the shore, is Peter's house, built much like Joseph's workshop but smaller. Before Jesus called him, Peter was a fisherman, here represented by two large fish painted on the front of his house. Between the house and the water is an entirely seaworthy aluminum rowboat resting on blocks. On the one hand, this adds to the fisherman theme. On the other hand, it no doubt provides a practical means for Holy Land USA personnel to take to the sea whenever the call comes, whether to scoop algae or to save a drowning tourist.

Also near the sea, among some trees just to the south, is Cana, where Jesus made a splash at a local wedding party by turning water into wine. Here Cana is represented by a large concrete pad, poured in the shape of a cross, along which several dozen concrete blocks have been arranged in rows for seating. Mike told me that wedding

Zacchaeus, Holy Land USA

ceremonies are often held here. Given the conservative evangelical orientation of this place, I doubt there's much wine flowing at them.

Departing Galilee, the road turns south and runs along the west side of the Jordan valley toward Jerusalem. On the way, I spied another cutout figure standing on the branch of a tree. It was Zacchaeus, the little man of ill-gotten riches who climbed a sycamore tree to see Jesus as he passed by. "Come down," Jesus commanded, "for today I must abide at thy house," after which Zacchaeus gave half of his riches to the poor and repaid those he had cheated fourfold (Luke 19). There are lots of sycamores in Holy Land USA, and Mr. Johnson took care to place him in one. However, I suspect his prime trailside location was more important than finding him the biblically correct tree species.

As we passed Zacchaeus in our little rolling tour, I wondered why he had been included in the Gospel story world we were traversing. It occurred to me that in relation to him, we would be part of Jesus's entourage. We were leaving Jesus's hometown with our faces set toward Jerusalem. He was looking on from the side of the road as we passed. Yet, on another level, we were expected to identify *with* Zacchaeus, trying to catch a glimpse of this man Jesus, to wrest a blessing, to have an encounter with the holy one of Israel.

Just before entering Jerusalem we made a stop at the Dome of the Rock, on Mount Moriah, where Abraham nearly sacrificed Isaac, and where Solomon later began building the Temple. A safety-railed footpath leads to the memorial Dome set atop a large rock mound. Surrounded by blue pillars made of painted oil drums, the centerpiece of the structure is a retired water tower. Openings have been cut through its thick steel wall, and inside is the Ark of the Lord, a wooden box, painted gold, topped with two jigsawed wings and the two tablets of the Ten Commandments.

"Amazing!" the older gentleman next to me exclaimed as we stood before the Ark. He turned to me and asked pointedly, "How did they come up with that?"

I wasn't entirely sure who he meant by "they." At first I thought he was referring to Mr. Johnson and his hired hands cutting through the thick wall of that water tank to put the Ark inside. But then I remembered that during Mike's opening welcome remarks, he had introduced me to the rest of the group as a biblical scholar. This man was asking me how the ancient Israelites "came up with that." For him, this wooden winged box and blow-torched water tower encircled by oil drums evoked the real thing. Not that he thought it was an entirely realistic representation, but it put him in the mind of the ancient Israelite Ark and tablets, and he saw this as an opportunity to ask someone who might know more.

"I really don't know," I said, shaking by head apologetically.

Next to the path leading up to the Dome is a neatly arranged stack of wood, recalling Abraham's near sacrifice of his son. GOD WILL PROVIDE THE LAMB, a nearby sign reads. Which is what Abraham told Isaac when he asked where the sacrificial animal was. But here I saw no ram caught in any nearby thicket. This might seem a serious omission, but I suspect it's intentional. In the evangelical Christian context of Holy Land USA, this absence refers visitors farther up the road to Calvary, where it is believed that God provided the ultimate sacrifice.

Not Quite There

"Amen. That's right. We're in Jerusalem now!" So we were. As we came down the valley into the Jerusalem area of Holy Land USA, the collective excitement of our group was palpable. All understood that this would be the culmination of the tour and of the story, in which we were participating as we moved along Journey Trail. We were approaching the salvific destination, the virtual heartland of the Christian faith, the place of Crucifixion and Resurrection. For many in our group, our kids included, Bedford County was less real than the Holy City itself.

Clover and I, however, were not quite there. We found ourselves unable to be fully present to this experience. On the one hand, we each have histories within evangelical circles that allowed us to

Empty Tomb, Holy Land USA

identify with our tour guide and travel companions. On the other hand, we no longer run in those circles, and that made us feel very much as outsiders.

As I mentioned earlier, I was raised with a strong sense of identity within conservative evangelical Christianity. Although I no longer identify with it, my childhood and teen years were steeped in that culture. You might say it remains a part of me even though I'm no longer a part of it.

Clover's religious background and experience left her, too, with one foot in the world of Holy Land USA and the other well outside it. Raised in a nonreligious family, she started attending a tiny "Bible-believing" Assembly of God church on the edge of her trailer park when she was eight years old. Her perfect attendance in Sunday school during that first year won her a scholarship to summer church camp. Over the years this little community of very loving and nurturing charismatic Christians became her home away from home and instilled in her a deep and abiding sense of identity as a loved child of God. When she went to college she lost touch with that little much-beloved community, but she remained heavily involved in similar (though somewhat less charismatic and less homespun) conservative evangelical Christian circles. It wasn't until she felt called to ordained ministry that she became alienated from those circles, in which the ordination of women is strongly opposed. Her sense of calling, along with an emerging feminist consciousness and orientation toward theologies of liberation, led her to break from that culture and hitch herself to the more progressive Presbyterian Church (USA).

Clover and I fell in love toward the end of college, in a philosophy of religion course, and within a couple years we were married and attending a Presbyterian seminary. As we've continued on our particular but closely entwined spiritual paths, I'd have to say that we've only grown more distant from our evangelical backgrounds. And yet, that particular and peculiar form of American Christianity remains very much a part of each of us. Like the Hotel California, you can check out any time you want but you can never really leave. It's in our blood. Its language, laced with phrases from the King James Bible and other classic Christian texts, constantly slips into our discourse—often in contexts where no one else hears it. It's our idiom, the theological pool in which our religious imaginations live and move and have their being. It's part of us, although we're no longer part of it. We're of its world but not in it.

Thus, on one level, we identified with our tour guide and travel companions. We knew the religious language and symbolism, understood the theological context, and we caught all the biblical references. On the other hand, we are no longer part of that tradition. Hearing it all as former insiders, defectors with no hard feelings, we responded with heartfelt appreciation for the sincerity of this world of experience but also with a distancing sense of irony and ambiguity. Reminded of the rich young ruler who sadly walked away from Jesus's calling, we felt a certain lonely unease at our incapacity to become part of the story with our travel companions.

Holy City

In Jerusalem proper, the main exhibit is an old two-story wooden building. Before the property was purchased for Holy Land USA, it had been the site of a government-operated still, and this building, near the stream (now known as the Jordan River), was the main base of operation. Now it's the Upper Room, where Jesus and his disciples shared a Passover Seder meal (the Last Supper) shortly before he was arrested and executed. Upstairs is a long table with thirteen stools, along with a Plexiglas-encased diorama of the scene of the Last Supper. Above the door, thirty coins with holes drilled through them are screwed to a sign to form a circle. Revealing a certain ironic sense of humor as it refers to the building's past and present significance, the words inside the circle read,

BETRAYAL
$TILL, A$ OF OLD.
MEN BY THEM$ELVES ARE PRICED.
FOR 30 PIECES
JUDA$ OLD, HIMELF.
NOT CHRIST.

(Notice there's no dollar sign in the name of Christ.)

Behind the still/Upper Room is the narrow trail marked by another sign:

VIA DOLOROSA

THE SORROWFUL WAY

THE ROUTE WHICH OUR LORD TRAVELED FROM THE

JUDGMENT SEAT OF PILATE,

TO THE PLACE OF HIS CRUCIFIXION ON MT. CALVARY.

MATT. 27:26–31

This Via Dolorosa, which has been modified to include a hand-operated mechanical conveyer for those who find this via too dolorous on foot, leads to a small flat area at the base of three tall, rough-hewn wooden crosses. Another narrow trail leads down and away from these crosses to a tomb cut into the rock beneath them. Inside is nothing but a wide stone bed, empty of course, illuminated by a single fluorescent light mounted into the rock ceiling.

Most of our fellow travelers milled about the Cross and empty tomb with apparent reverence. Everyone entered the tomb to see the empty stone bed for her- or himself. Mike didn't rush us. He left the Mr. Microphone in the truck and waited quietly among the trees near another large seating area of neatly arranged blocks. Clearly, he was used to visitors lingering at this place for a long time.

Clover and I noticed that one older woman remained at the foot of the central cross far longer than anyone else, while her daughter stood patiently by. She kneeled low to the ground, still, silent, eyes wide open and fixed on the foot of the Cross. Later on, back on the trailer, her daughter explained to Clover that she'd been going through a very difficult time in her life. There, facing the Cross, she had become suddenly overwhelmed by what Jesus had done for her. It was like she had been transported to the time and place of Jesus's Crucifixion. She was there.

Indeed, she wasn't the only one to have such an experience at Calvary that day. As Mike's truck pulled us down the last quarter mile of Journey Trail, away from Jerusalem and toward the bookstore and parking lot, the mood among our fellow travelers was one of solemn reflection.

Making It Real

Over the course of the tour, a remarkable transformation had occurred for many on board. They had become part of the story world of Holy Land USA. It had, in a very profound way, become real.

Granted, Holy Land USA is far from geographically or historically "realistic" in the common sense of the term. It doesn't realistically represent either the geography of Palestine and Israel or the historical world of first-century Judea during the time of Jesus. And yet, for many of our fellow travelers, it had become *profoundly, phenomenally real*. But "real" in a sense very different from what we mean by empirically or objectively real. Real, rather, in the sense of being religiously real, an experience of ultimate reality. Real in the sense that one feels as though one has become a part of it. As though one has lost oneself in it. For the woman at the foot of the Cross, as for many others, normal, everyday time and space had been suspended, and the story world of Holy Land USA had become reality. She was *there*.

What made this possible? How did Holy Land USA succeed in hosting such a religious experience for so many? How did it become religiously real? I see three particular ways by which Holy Land USA works to create an experience of the "real" for its visitors: first, its rhetoric of accuracy; second, its narrative arrangement of space; and third, its creation of a wilderness experience. Let me say a bit about each of these in turn.

First, Holy Land USA succeeded in making itself religiously real to visitors by deploying an extensive *rhetoric of accuracy* and historical realism. Mike frequently referred to the ratios used for laying out the land as a scaled-down version of the Holy Land, and on several occasions he mentioned that Bob Johnson had taken great care to locate and build all his exhibits according to the exact measurements he had taken from the original sites in Israel. And there were signs that reiterated Mike's points. Near Calvary and the empty tomb, for example, one sign read

> CALVARY — EMPTY TOMB
> THESE ARE JUST AS REALISTIC
> AS IF YOU WERE ACTUALLY THERE.

Mike also cited the testimonies of former tourists, ministers, and biblical scholars who had visited the actual site in Israel and who verified that this display is a most accurate representation. Indeed, Mike said that several visitors had told him that this display was actually *better* than the original because the original was so overrun with tourists, security guards, and gift shops. The implication was that this copy is in some sense *more real* that the original, that is, more directly available to experience.

The rhetoric of accuracy and realism is important for creating this experience of the "real" Holy Land here. But more important, I think, is its *narrative arrangement of space*. As mentioned earlier, this is a story-shaped world, an inhabitable story. Guests don't rove the area at will. There is a beginning and an end to their experience of this space. Journey Trail is a one-way trip that walks or drives guests through a certain version of the story of Jesus, from birth to ministry to death to Resurrection. As guests progress through the space of Holy Land USA, then, they also progress through the Gospel story that is mapped onto it. As they go deeper into the space, they go deeper into the story. By the time they arrive at Jerusalem, the Gospel narrative and Journey Trail have converged into a single sacred story world, and they have become part of it.

In this respect, Holy Land USA may be understood as something of an American evangelical form of pilgrimage, what anthropologists of religion Victor and Edith Turner describe in *Image and Pilgrimage in Christian Culture* as "a complex surrogate for the journey to the source and heartland of the faith." Indeed, it is strikingly similar to traditional European Catholic pilgrimage sites. As with those sites, Holy Land USA was created so that locals of modest means could experience the land of the Bible, especially Jerusalem, without needing to travel abroad. And as with those traditional pilgrimages, the experience here is treated as a kind of individual rite of initiation. Because, as Mike puts it, "Christian faith has its roots in Israel," it is believed that every Christian should make this transformative journey of faith to the heart of the Holy Land. Even if she takes the journey as part of a group, moreover, she ultimately faces Calvary alone. Finally, as with traditional Catholic pilgrimages, toward the end of the journey (in this case Jerusalem), the pilgrim encounters a concentration of sacred objects and symbolic structures (e.g., Upper Room, Calvary, empty tomb, prolific signage). Thus, as the pilgrim reaches the culmination of the journey, her own subjectivity is increasingly enveloped in the sacred world, signifying her newfound freedom from the mundane order of the everyday, profane world.

In this light, we might see Holy Land USA as a kind of return of the repressed within American evangelicalism, which has tended to define itself over against Catholicism and Orthodox Christianity by avoiding, if not outright condemning, all forms of material religion, ritual embodiment, and sacramental theology. Indeed, Protestant tradition has been particularly critical of pilgrimage. The great

Protestant theologian and father of the Reformation John Calvin frequently referred to pilgrimage as one of the most egregious examples of the corruption of Roman Catholicism by its priesthood. In chapter thirteen of his *Institutes of the Christian Religion*, he reckoned it as a form of idolatry on account of its attachment to material things, "not only empty and nugatory, but full of manifest impiety," a form of "fictitious worship" abhorred by God.

As deeply Protestant as it is, Holy Land USA is nonetheless a kind of pilgrimage space, speaking to a certain desire to inhabit and traverse the sacred story, to encounter the holy in material form, and thereby to experience a kind of biblical literacy quite different from the kind preached from the pulpits of evangelical churches and studied in Friday prayer breakfasts at Denny's. Here is a form of biblical literacy that must be embodied, and that requires one to come to an experience of certain material objects and spaces as sacramental.

Part of what makes Holy Land USA work, I think, has to do with the tension that exists within this place between the *rhetoric* of accuracy and realism, discussed earlier, and the highly *unrealistic* and *historically inaccurate* objects and spaces one sees everywhere. Recall the nineteenth-century farm equipment, the prevalence of concrete, the oil drums and water tank, the still, and, above all, the two-dimensional plywood cutout figures that populate nearly every site. None of this jibes with the continual assertions of realism. Yet, as the traveler moves through the space and therefore through the biblical narrative mapped onto it, she forgets or at least overlooks their anachronicity and flatness. They are accepted as real. What is initially seen as unrealistic eventually comes to conform to what is *said* by Mike and the various signs, thanks to the *narrative development* of the traveler's experience as she moves through this space. In this respect, the unrealism of objects like the cutout figures is, paradoxically, important to the process of coming to experience of the "real"

Holy Land in this place. We might compare this dynamic to the theater experience, in which a degree of unreality is important to the audience's imaginative participation in the story world of the play. The experience of theatrical drama as real often depends on more or less unrealistic stagecraft: a stage, two-dimensional facades and other backdrops, makeup, and costuming. As the narrative drama progresses, the audience becomes less and less aware of that lack of realism. At the same time they become less and less aware of the distance between them and their everyday world on the one hand and the actors and their story world on the other.

The affective experience of the really real at Holy Land USA works, then, as a result of its *disarrangement* of expected meanings: its placement of preindustrial plows and tractor wheels in Joseph's workshop; or its placement of the Upper Room in a whiskey still; its placement of biblical Israel and Calvary in the Blue Ridge Mountains of Virginia. All of these are disarrangements as much as arrangements. They don't sit well at the beginning of the journey. They "cross conceptual wires," as Clifford Geertz puts it in his essay on "Deep Play," so that "phenomena...are clothed in signifiers which normally point to other referents." Yet as the story and the tour progress, the disarrangement opens the possibility of a new arrangement, one that allows travelers a truly novel experience, namely, an experience of the Holy Land.

There is, I think, a third means by which this place lends itself to such profound religious experiences among its visitors. It has to do with its subtitle, "A Nature Sanctuary." Let's call it the *wilderness experience* of Holy Land USA.

On first blush it seems odd to put the land of the Bible among the foothills of the Blue Ridge Mountains. That part of the country is not exactly reminiscent of Israel-Palestine, past or present. Seeing a creek trickling around large mossy boulders beneath white oaks and tall mountain pines doesn't quite call the Jordan River to mind. And spying a white-tailed deer just behind an old whiskey still doesn't quite recall the Last Supper in the Upper Room.

Yet, in another sense, it all works. The ecological disconnect between this natural landscape and that of the Middle East doesn't present itself as an obstacle for visitors. I think that this is the case because this setting does something else for guests, something ultimately more important for hosting their religious experience. That is, it removes them from their day-to-day life and places them in a wilderness context.

In fact, the wilderness excursion has deep significance within biblical religious tradition. There the wilderness figures as a chaotic, unformed place of new beginnings. Think of Moses, Elijah, David, and Jesus. Each returns from the wilderness transformed, ready to take on new lives of leadership in the community. Think as well of the Israelites themselves, who leave Egypt and enter the wilderness as a band of runaway Hebrew slaves and eventually enter the Promised Land as God's chosen nation. Think too of the early monks who went into the wilderness to purge themselves of worldly concerns and purify their lives for devotion to God. And, stretching a little (not far) beyond traditional religion into the less explicitly religious traditions of American romanticism, think of Jack London and countless American nature writers for whom the wilderness signifies a place of personal transformation and rebirth. Like the waters of chaos from which the world was born, the wilderness is a locus of potential, a place of fecund depth.

The nature sanctuary aspect of Holy Land USA, then, is not simply a nod to the will of Mr. Johnson's late son. Rather, it provides visitors with a kind of otherworldly "wilderness experience" that becomes the context for bringing about a deeper, more "real," more powerfully transformative religious encounter.

As wilderness experience and as pilgrimage, Holy Land USA may be understood in terms of what religionists call a liminal phenomenon. Liminal, from the Latin *limen*, basically means "threshold." Religious anthropologist Arnold van Gennep developed the concept of the liminal in religious ritual to describe times and spaces of transition from one state to another, threshold experiences such as rites of passage. Although not "liminal" in the full sense developed by van Gennep, Holy Land USA is something of a "symbolic and spatial area of transition," as he puts it. As it is traversed within the ritual process of the tour, it is intended to bring about a personal transformation in the pilgrim/tourist, so that she exits that space a new person, having seen the Holy Land, having been there at the foot of the Cross, and having witnessed the stone rolled away from the empty tomb.

Ascension

Earlier I indicated that Journey Trail ends at the empty tomb. That's not exactly right. A few hundred yards south of Jerusalem, just before visitors return to the bookstore and parking lot, the tour makes another stop near a large grassy hill. Lying along its carefully mown face is a huge cross made of white painted boulders. On one side, written in large concrete blocks, are the words, MT. OLIVET, and on the other side are the words, JESUS ASCENDED / ACTS — 1. Here is Holy Land USA's version of the place of Christ's ascension. But look a little more closely at the grassy area at the top of the hill. You'll notice several other large stones. These spell nothing. They are gravestones. People are buried up there. That's right, you can be baptized in the Jordan, get married in Cana, and be buried on Mount Olivet. Apparently some have had a real enough experience to decide they want to rest here, in this Holy Land, the virtual land of their biblical ancestors. Now, on first blush, making Mount Olivet into a burial ground may not seem to jibe with the ascension theme. Yet for those who confess the resurrection of the body and the life everlasting, what better place to lie in wait for the Second Coming than where Christ went up the first time around? "Amen."

Clover and I weren't about to purchase a family plot. But as we rolled past, we understood how others might.

Chapter Two

MAGIC KINGDOM COME

*The Holy Land Experience
Orlando, Florida*

"When are they doing the Crucifixion?" a middle-aged man in a yellow plastic poncho asked the gift shop cashier as he nudged past me in the check-out line, his wife and embarrassed teenage son in tow. The thunderclaps and drumming of the rain on the roof were growing louder. A crowd of a hundred or more tourists were gathered, their cameras flashing, around a large model replica of ancient Jerusalem near the other end of the room as a silver-haired man in an Indiana Jones outfit, complete with safari hat pinned up on one side, began lecturing on what the city was like around 66 CE, before the destruction of the Temple by the Romans. The man at the cash register wasn't interested.

"We drove all the way to Orlando from Little Rock just to see the Crucifixion. It's the most famous part of Holy Land Experience. Is it gonna be on time? At the Tabernacle show they said the Crucifixion would happen here in the Shofar building at twelve forty-five."

"Well sir," the cashier explained, "they can't do the Crucifixion outside today on account of the lightning. He can't get on that cross way up high like that in this weather. It's too dangerous. He could get electrocuted. So they had to bring the show inside today, over there in the Shofar Auditorium." She pointed across the gift shop display area to the double doors that opened onto a high-school-size auditorium, now empty except for a stagehand wrapping up micro-phone cords. "And that show just finished."

"Yeah, we saw that. It was just a few people in costumes singing and then a talk. No Crucifixion. No Cross or anything like that."

"That's right, sir. They can't get the Cross into the auditorium. It's too big and heavy to move in there. It wouldn't even fit through the doors. Plus it's permanently mounted on top of the Calvary exhibit outside. So they can only do the music and lecture parts in there. But," she added cheerily, "the weather is sure to clear. This storm will pass, and there'll be plenty of other outdoor shows to see this afternoon."

"*No Crucifixion?*" he all but shouted, leaning over the counter. He turned to me, crestfallen, expecting the news to hit me with the same terrible force.

I shrugged helplessly, thinking to myself how real life sometimes imitates *Monty Python,* and showed him the DVD I was about to purchase. "You can have it on video, anyway," I offered.

He wasn't impressed. "We could see that just as well at home. We came here for the real thing."

"Oh well," he muttered to his family as they pulled their poncho hoods over their heads and shuffled out the door and into the pour-ing rain. "I guess we might as well see what else there is."

The cashier was right on both counts. The storm soon cleared, as Florida storms almost always do, and the Holy Land Experience is so much more than a daily Crucifixion show. A few miles up the in-terstate from Disney World and Universal Studios, the Holy Land Experience is a $16 million, fifteen-acre "living biblical history mu-seum" that claims in its highly polished publicity materials to repre-sent "in elaborate and authentic detail the city of Jerusalem and its religious importance between the years 1450 BC and AD 66 (through the Old and New Testaments, from Genesis through Revelation)."

It aims to create "a total sensory experience that is educational, historical, theatrical, inspirational and evangelistic, blending sights, sounds and tastes that transport guests 7,000 miles away and more than 3,000 years back in time."

On a peak-season weekend day, the Holy Land Experience hosts well over a thousand visitors, nearly all of them conservative Protestant Christians. For many it has become a popular alternative to the theme parks operated by Disney, which the Southern Baptists, Assemblies of God, and other conservative Christian groups have boycotted on account of its support of "Gay Day" and its progressive partner benefits for gay employees.

The theological and entrepreneurial genius behind the Holy Land Experience is the Reverend Marvin J. Rosenthal. Raised in a Conservative Jewish family in Philadelphia, he converted to Christianity as a teenager through a relationship with a pair of Christian missionaries who used to visit his family's neighborhood store. Then, as he tells his own story, he fled God and his calling to ministry for eighteen years, serving in the Marine Corps and working as a professional dancer, among other things. Eventually, in 1965, he went to seminary at Dallas Theological Seminary, a conservative school well known among Protestant evangelicals, and was ordained as a Baptist minister.

Rev. Rosenthal described himself to me as a "builder." While in the pastorate he was responsible for several building campaigns, but the Holy Land Experience is his pièce de résistance. This project began in the early 1990s, after a painful separation from a large congregation in Texas on account of theological differences concerning what will happen to Christians during the end-times tribulation. He had been taking groups of Christians to Israel for many years, and began imagining how he might create a place in America that could give people a virtual experience of the Holy Land. Although Orlando was not on his original short list of potential sites, his friends and colleagues insisted that it was ideal. Soon enough he was persuaded. He and his wife moved into a rental home there and began plans for the Holy Land Experience. The first phase, which took four years to complete, involved building office space and a scale model of Jerusalem inspired by the model in the lobby of the Holy Land Hotel in the city of Jerusalem. At that point he was able to establish a company and start an effective fundraising campaign to landscape the property and build its numerous large exhibits, including a model of the Jerusalem Temple, Calvary and the Garden Tomb, a Wilderness Tabernacle, a Jerusalem street market, gift shops, a theater, a café, and a Scriptorium to house a private collection of ancient manuscripts and artifacts. In February 2001, the Holy Land Experience opened its doors to visitors, promising to transport them back through time for a firsthand exploration of "the world of the Bible."

Rev. Rosenthal's ministry has been dominated by three interests: to teach Christians about the history and ritual practices of ancient Israel and contemporary Judaism; to promote a particular theological understanding of what will happen during the end times; and to lead Jews to convert to Christianity. These interests might not initially appear to have much to do with each other. Yet, as we will see, they are the triple pillars of the Holy Land Experience.

Holy Disneyland Experience

Although the Holy Land Experience is another example of biblical recreation, it is worlds away from the blue highways and Blue Ridge Mountains of Holy Land USA. Indeed, it's almost as far from that world of homespun hospitality and personal piety as twenty-first-century Disney World is from first-century Nazareth. The Holy Land

City Gate, The Holy Land Experience

Experience is a fundamentalist Magic Kingdom, a Disneyesque alternative to Disney World.

As we drove into the sprawling, perfectly paved parking lot, marked off from the main road by a row of pillars and an archway presumably meant to recall Roman ruins, it was clear that we weren't in Virginia anymore. And clearer still when we purchased tickets, which were not *quite* as pricey as Disney attractions. We wouldn't have been altogether surprised had we heard music piped into the parking lot—perhaps the evangelical equivalent of "It's a Small World after All."

It was August of 2003, a year after our first family road trip in *Home-a-Roam*, and less than three months since George W. Bush had announced the end of major combat with Iraq and the beginning of the occupation. Anyone with a military identification was getting free admission to the Holy Land Experience. Whether that drew more than the usual numbers of war-supporting patriots I can't say, but there were lots of bumper stickers with American flags and pro-war slogans ("These colors don't run").

Tickets in hand, we joined the growing lines of visitors filing through a pair of subway-like turnstiles under the City Gate, an imposing gray faux stone structure modeled on the Damascus and Lion's Gates of Jerusalem. A woman dressed as a first-century Palestinian peasant showed us where to insert our tickets after a couple of very twenty-first century security guards with walkie-talkies had finished searching our bags.

On the faces of kids, parents, and grandparents entering the Holy City was that strange mix of anxious anticipation and preemptory boredom, eagerness and exhaustion so familiar to anyone who has "vacationed" in Orlando, where each day's attraction promises to be the greatest spectacle of all. Indeed, the crowds looked like your typical Universal Studios or Disney World demographic except for the prevalence of T-shirts with evangelical messages, from the very common "God bless America" to the more clever varieties that take a second to get, like "Church building began with two nails in the hands of a carpenter."

Once through the City Gate, we found ourselves in the Jerusalem Street Market, advertised as a "fascinating, 2,000-year-old Middle Eastern marketplace" where guests are encouraged to visit with local street merchants (I didn't see any) and browse in two gift shops, a bookstore called The Old Scroll Shop and a souvenir store called Methuselah's Mosaics. The shops were stocked with plenty of the expected theme park memorabilia—coffee cups, T-shirts, and so on—with images of the Holy Land Experience on them. But there were also many items with Jewish themes: Israeli-made clothing, shofars, menorahs, yarmulkes, books about ancient Israelite festivals, and how-to guides for incorporating Jewish religious rituals into Christian life.

As we wandered around the store, my daughter, Sophie, whispered to me, "My Jewish friends sure would feel uncomfortable here."

"What makes you say that just now?"

"Well, like, there's all this Jewish stuff, but this place is so Christian. Nobody but a certain kind of Christian would be comfortable here. I don't. I feel like they shouldn't have all this stuff." What she was picking up on, I believe, was a kind of Christian co-opting of Judaism that was clearly operative here. Of course, Christianity began as a Jewish movement (the "Jesus movement"), and many, including myself, believe that Christianity needs to learn more from its parent religion. But here the feeling was more along the lines of supersessionism, that is, the ideology that Christianity is a truer form of Judaism than Judaism itself, and therefore it is the true heir of God's promise. Moreover, history has taught Jewish people to be wary of Christian fascination with and enthusiastic embrace of Judaism. Rightly so, for such evangelical Judeophilia often has a hostile flipside, revealed only when it becomes clear that Jews aren't about to convert. A place like the Holy Land Experience, then, raises a lot of big red flags for Jews and for those of us concerned about the persistence of anti-Jewish tendencies within Christianity.

Sophie is surely right about how her Jewish friends would feel here. In fact, I was surprised to realize, after our visit, that a number of my Jewish friends (some of whom are the parents of Sophie's friends) knew about this place and were repulsed by its very concept. They had read about Rosenthal's interest in using the park as a means of proselytizing to Jews, and about Jewish and Christian protests demanding that these aims be made more explicit.

Despite the park's refusal to make such proselytizing intentions explicit, most Jews are steering clear. As mentioned earlier, the vast majority of visitors are conservative Christians. But the intention behind the fascination with Judaism and Jewish ritual is not only evangelical. As we will see, it is also and especially apocalyptic.

In the open area outside the gift shops, a friendly couple dressed as shepherds were luring children with kid goats. The man had a tall wood staff and was posing for pictures. The scene reminded me of a cross between a county fair petting area and a church Christmas pageant, which is the only other place I've ever seen adults wearing shepherd outfits. Here and elsewhere, the presence of live actors portraying certain roles drawn from first-century Jerusalem adds a certain Colonial Williamsburg flavor to this Christian Magic Kingdom.

In addition to the Jerusalem Street Market, the Holy Land Experience includes four major replicas of ancient Israelite or Judean sacred sites, each of which serves as the venue for theatrical performances that take place at certain times each day. The largest and most prominent is the Temple of the Great King, a six-story, half-scale replica of the first-century Jerusalem Temple, the so-called third temple that was begun under the reign of Herod the Great and completed in 64 CE. In front is the spacious Plaza of the Nations, surrounded by thirty Roman columns. The Temple stairs serve as the stage for the first show of the morning, "Today's the Day," a musical drama in which a group of everyday Jerusalemites sing out on state-of-the-art wireless microphones about their hopes and longings for the coming of the Messiah. Among them was Simeon, the one in the Gospel of Luke who, along with the prophetess Anna, first recognized Jesus as the Messiah when his parents presented him at the Temple. (Seth, who knew the story from Sunday school, pointed out later that Anna appeared to be missing from this production.) As the voices rose and converged in a collective crescendo during the final number, someone offstage released a dozen or so doves, which fluttered about for a few seconds to much applause from the audience.

Just south of the Temple is Qumran Cave, a lumpy mound of sculpted orange-brown plastic somewhat reminiscent of a rocky hill. This serves as the stage for "The Ministry of Jesus," who preaches selections from the Sermon on the Mount and performs healings. Eventually, the interior of this mound will house an exhibit about the Dead Sea Scrolls. I would expect that this exhibit will promote the view (entirely erroneous, most scholars agree) that certain passages in the scrolls testify to Jesus as the Jewish Messiah.

Between Qumran Cave and the pond that separates the Holy Land Experience from the parking lot is Calvary's Garden Tomb, another sculpted orange formation with the standard three-cross arrangement rising from the mound above it. This, of course, is the stage for the famous Crucifixion reenactment that, much to the chagrin of my friend from Arkansas, sometimes must be canceled due to weather. In this show, a very bloodied Jesus is raised high on the Cross by snarling, chiding Roman centurions as the audience watches from the garden area below. Throughout the dramatization, the songs sung by the two Marys and the disciples emphasize that this must happen as a sacrificial atonement for the sins of the world, a theme that is most prominent in the Gospel of John, the foundational biblical text for most evangelical Christians. Interestingly, and commendably, in this Passion play, Jewish leaders and crowds don't play the negative role of Jesus's conspiring accusers and antagonists, as they so often do in other renditions (Mel Gibson's *The Passion of the Christ* being the most recent example).

Early in the morning, before the rains began, I had noticed a Roman centurion up on Calvary, guarding the Crucifixion area—a nonverbal promotion for the show scheduled later in the day. He was handsomely decked out in crimson cloth, plumed helmet, golden armor, and studded leather. He paced back and forth at the foot of the crosses, staring coldly at anyone below whose eye he could catch. When I pointed my camera at him, he quickly struck a well-rehearsed Napoleon-like profile pose, chin up, chest out, hand on his hilt.

At the base of Calvary Hill is the empty tomb, a small cave surrounded by a nicely landscaped rest area with benches, flowers, and neatly trimmed hedges. Next to the opening, behold, a well-rounded artificial stone, rolled away. There are two tombs in Jerusalem that claim to have been the site of Jesus's burial, the one at the Church of the Holy Sepulcher and the Garden Tomb. Scholars disagree as to which, if either, is the right one. The Holy Land Experience opted for the latter, based in part on Jesus's post-Resurrection visit with Mary in the Gospel of John, in which she initially mistakes him for the gardener. Beyond this biblical justification, the garden spot provides a quiet space for reflection by visitors. Indeed, throughout the day, even in lightning and pouring rain, people milled around the tomb area, waiting for a quiet moment alone to pray, or pose for a picture.

To the east of Qumran Cave, closest to the interstate, is the Wilderness Tabernacle, a replica of the moveable tent in which the ancient Hebrews carried out priestly rites during their forty years of wandering in the wilderness. Here visitors enjoy a climate-controlled dramatic demonstration of the annual Yom Kippur sacrifice, performed on the half hour throughout the day. Sitting reverently on bleachers in a dark room, the audience watches the shadowy silhouette of a bearded, ephod-clad high priest inside the illuminated holy of holies in the back of the tent as he carries out his various rites in order to call down the divine presence.

Throughout the history of biblical recreation in America, Tabernacle replicas built according to the biblical directions given by God to Moses in the book of Exodus have proven particularly popular. Why? Let me suggest one likely reason. In the biblical story of Exodus, building the Tabernacle is the means by which the Hebrew people host God's glorious presence in the wilderness. As soon as the Tabernacle is completed exactly according to God's directions, God's presence descends in a cloud and fills it (Exodus 40). The precise and careful re-creation of the Tabernacle according to biblical specs, then, in some sense, has at least the symbolic meaning of hosting divine presence. Build it and God will come. What makes the Holy Land Experience's Tabernacle somewhat unique is that the emphasis appears to be less on the actual physical structure and more on the ritual practices performed in it.

Another reason is that the Yom Kippur sacrifice performed in the Tabernacle is often interpreted by Christians as a foreshadowing of the eventual sacrifice of God's son, Jesus Christ, for the sins of all humanity. This meaning is explicitly given in the Holy Land Experience performance: as it concludes, the recorded voice of the priest wonders aloud whether this once-a-year sacrifice for the expiation of the people's sins might be but a rehearsal for an ultimate sacrifice yet to come, one that would atone for all time. This meaning does not, however, account for the great detail included in this particular performance of the Yom Kippur rite. For that, we'll need to look into the Holy Land Experience's interest not only in the Israelite past but in the apocalyptic future.

The imaginary geography created by these major sites of biblical recreation at the Holy Land Experience is closer to Disney World than to Holy Land USA. The Holy Land Experience reflects little effort to replicate the geographical space of the land of Israel or Jerusalem. The main sites here are clustered together in ways that do not reflect their relative locations in Israel and Palestine. Next to the Temple is Qumran Cave (far from Jerusalem in Israel), and on the other side of Qumran is Calvary's Garden Tomb. Unlike Holy Land USA, moreover, the Holy Land Experience ignores the natural landmarks of Israel and Palestine altogether. There is no Jordan River, no Sea of Galilee, no Dead Sea. The beautifully landscaped pond on the property bears no reference to any body of water from the "land of the Bible." Nor does the Holy Land Experience re-create biblical time in any coherent, integrated way. The Wilderness Tabernacle and the Herodian Temple, separated by centuries in Israelite and Judean history, are right next to each other. Each site is isolated from the others by walls, hedges and other barriers so that when you are in one, you are cut off from the sights and sounds of the others, much like the *Men in Black* ride experience is isolated from the *ET* ride experience at Universal Studios. Unlike Holy Land USA, then, there is no guided tour through a biblical narrative space. In fact, there is no single, coherent narrative space. The place reads like a collection of biblical passages or scenes, presented in no particular sequential order, so that each can be experienced independently of the others.

There are two other major buildings on the premises: the Shofar Auditorium building, which also houses administrative offices, another gift shop, and Rev. Rosenthal's original Jerusalem model; and the Scriptorium, home of the Center for Biblical Antiquities, a private collection of biblical manuscripts and artifacts organized into a walk-through tour. On first impression it might seem that this collection, which was offered to Rev. Rosenthal early on in his building campaign, is out of place at the Holy Land Experience, since it has nothing to do with re-creating the places and stories of the Bible. But in fact it is central, even foundational, to the place in that it lends authenticity and veracity to the other more dramatic elements. A museum about the history of scripture, it functions symbolically as the biblical anchor of the entire place. It has the effect of grounding all the contemporary musical drama and Disney-esque landscaping in scripture and history. Even if you don't visit it, just knowing it's there gives a *feeling* of biblical depth to what otherwise could quickly begin to seem superficial. In this respect its subtitle, Center for Biblical Antiquity, is more than revealing of its intended function, which is to *center* this fantastical place in biblical antiquity.

While the "This Is the Day" cast of first-century messianic Jews performed their show tunes on the Temple stairs, I stole away to wander the grounds alone, pondering it all in my heart. As I turned a corner on my way to the Oasis Palms Café and Caravan Cabana, where a couple of visitors were washing down Goliath Burgers with Sierra Mists, I nearly stepped on the toes of a leper resting against a post. He was wrapped head to knee in tattered cloth and bandages splattered with drops of red. His face was covered by a hood with two eye holes cut into it like a last-minute Halloween ghost costume. I had caught him off guard, out of character, taking a break in the shade like anyone, with or without leprosy, would want to do on a hot June day in Orlando.

"Do you mind if I take your picture?" I asked, and he immediately struck his well-rehearsed pose, holding out his hands toward me, as if begging for...food, money, a healing touch, a raise.

Around the next corner I bumped into two centurions, one of whom I recognized as the guard at the foot of the Cross. I later learned that they were waiting for their cue to interrupt the messianic expectations of Simeon and company on the Temple stairs. At the moment they appeared to be guarding the Main Service Disconnect emergency switch on the wall behind them. This time I didn't bother asking permission to take a picture. I aimed my camera and they immediately struck their poses, brandishing swords, makeup scars, and downright un-Christian scowls. "Can you show

Leper, The Holy Land Experience

me how to get to the Shofar Auditorium?" I asked the slightly kinder-looking one. Without speaking he drew near, staring coldly, and, like the Ghost of Christmas Future, pointed an outstretched arm down the walkway to the north. I didn't dare ask him to sign my scrapbook.

Holy Prewrath Rapture

The Holy Land Experience is a strange brew. On the one hand, it's a Disney-like world of spectacular attractions meant to wow visitors with high-end stagecraft and costuming. On the other hand, like Colonial Williamsburg with its early American character actors demonstrating how to dip a candle or load a black powder rifle, the Holy Land Experience is an educational site focused intently on teaching Christians about Israelite and Judean history, rituals, and festivals. It's Christian edutainment.

The most prominent example of this fascination with ancient Israel was the dramatic presentation of the Yom Kippur sacrifice of atonement in the Wilderness Tabernacle. As mentioned earlier, this annual sacrifice of atonement for the sins of Israel is believed by evangelicals to be important as a foreshadowing of the later atoning sacrifice of Jesus Christ for the sins of humanity once and for all. Yet I was struck by the elaborate detail of the presentation, which was above and beyond the usual Christian interest in this particular ancient rite. Likewise in the Old Scroll Shop and Methuselah's Mosaics, the prevalence of Israel souvenirs, educational literature about Jewish festivals and rituals, and even ritual objects like shofars and menorahs indicated an unusually enthusiastic interest in ancient Israelite and contemporary Jewish ritual practices.

There is indeed something more riding on the Holy Land Experience than the desire to give visitors a virtual experience of the land of the Bible. Beneath the explicit aim of giving guests a glimpse of life during biblical times is a far more zealous ideological interest in promoting a very specific biblical theology of the end times, one in which knowledge of Israelite ritual practices, especially those associated with the Jerusalem Temple, is foundational.

This apocalyptic theology is less explicit in the various theatrical

Centurions, The Holy Land Experience

presentations and lectures than in Rev. Rosenthal's larger ministry
movement, Zion's Hope Inc., of which the Holy Land Experience is
the most popular and public part. Based in the offices of the Shofar
building, Zion's Hope publishes the magazine *Zion's Fire* and books
of apocalyptic theology based on reading the Bible, especially the

book of Revelation, as a scriptural code that allows the faithful to decipher precisely how the coming of the Antichrist, the Rapture, divine judgment, and Christ's Second Coming will take place.

Or is it first the Rapture, then the Antichrist, then divine judgment, then the Second Coming? Or maybe is it first the Antichrist, then divine judgment, then the Second Coming, then the Rapture? These are the kinds of questions that keep end-times-oriented Christians tossing and turning on Saturday nights and arguing and splintering on Sunday mornings. When they see the bumper sticker, IN CASE OF RAPTURE, THIS VEHICLE WILL BE UNMANNED, they wonder whether the driver thinks the Antichrist will be around at that point to see the traffic catastrophe that will ensue.

Let me offer a brief outsider's view of the lay of the end-times land among conservative evangelical and fundamentalist Christians. There are three main camps: pretribulationist, or "pretrib"; posttrib; and prewrath. Each is armed with an arsenal of biblical proof texts and each accuses the others of twisting holy scriptures to serve their own wishful thinking. In an apocalyptic nutshell, *pretribs* argue that the Rapture will occur *before* seven years of tribulation, including the time of the Antichrist and the time of God's wrathful judgment on the Earth. Christians will be taken up before all that happens and will watch from heaven, out of harm's way. The Second Coming will happen after the divine judgment, at which point Christians will return to Earth along with Christ who will reign from the New Jerusalem for a thousand years. *Posttribs* argue that the Rapture will occur after the seven years of tribulation. Christians will remain on Earth throughout that time. For them the Rapture and the Second Coming are simultaneous. Finally, *prewraths* argue that the faithful will undergo the first part of the tribulation, inflicted by the Antichrist, symbolized by the first six seals in the book of

Revelation, but will not undergo the ultimate divine wrath and judgment on Earth, symbolized by the seventh seal. The Rapture will happen during the tribulation but before the divine wrath.

In my own upbringing within evangelical Christianity, I had few direct encounters with apocalyptic theology, pre- or post-anything. Like most youth groups in these circles, ours would sometimes sing the popular Larry Norman song "I Wish We'd All Been Ready" ("There's no time to change your mind, the Son has come, and you've been left behind," we all crooned, long-faced). And we watched the 1970s end-times movie series produced by Mark IV films—*A Thief in the Night* (1972), *A Distant Thunder* (1977), and *Image of the Beast* (1981). (A fourth, *The Prodigal Planet* [1983], came out after I'd left for college and left those circles behind.) Some of my high-school friends seriously considered forgoing college, because they felt that the end was near and that there might be better things to do with one's time. And once for Christmas I gave my dad a copy of *The Late Great Planet Earth*, by archconservative Cold War end-times guru Hal Lindsey. But I never read it, and I don't think dad read it with any great interest or enthusiasm. In fact, neither of my parents took much cop in the various theories of when, where, and how that swirled around some Bible study circles in our community. They felt that such things were better left to God. If even Jesus said neither he nor the angels in heaven know the day or the hour, they felt, what makes others think they do know?

I share this bit from my own background because it's important to recognize that not all conservative, evangelical, and/or fundamentalist Christians care one iota about these debates. Too often those who don't identify with any of these strains of Christian thought lump them all together—usually as "fundamentalist"—and assume that they all are obsessed with end-times theology. Indeed, that's precisely the disconnect between the Holy Land Experience and many of its visitors. They may be conservative and/or evangelical and/or fundamentalist, but they are not necessarily keen to nail down the specifics of the Second Coming.

In any case, Rosenthal's Zion's Hope Inc. is prewrath all the way. In fact, Rosenthal is well-known in conservative Christian circles as the main proponent of the prewrath argument. And a central goal of Rosenthal's books and magazine is to promote his position. So too his latest work, the Holy Land Experience.

At the heart of the Holy Land Experience is not simply the desire to evangelize Jewish people. That certainly is a goal, but most Jews will never set foot on these grounds. Rather, as a Christian Zionist ministry, its primary drive appears to be to educate gentile Christians about Israel, Judaism, and Jewish ritual practices, especially those of the ancient Jerusalem Temple. Why? Because they believe that in the final days Jerusalem will be restored to the Jews, and that the Temple, which was destroyed by the Romans in 70 CE, will be rebuilt and its ancient sacrificial practices (most prominent among them being Yom Kippur) reinstated. This restoration of the Temple and its sacrifices is considered to be the necessary precursor to and sure sign of the immanent Second Coming. So learning about ancient Israelite sacrificial practices, and learning about Jerusalem and its Temple, are not just matters of historical interest. They need to be studied because they will be restored and will play a part in the end times, the fulfillment of God's salvation history.

Behind the stucco walls, tapestry curtains, and office doors of this evangelical Magic Kingdom is a particular Christian Zionist vision of Kingdom Come. The retellings and reenactments performed at the Holy Land Experience are forms of apocalyptic expectation. Here one is meant to experience the past in order to anticipate the future.

Needless to say, I didn't respond well to the Holy Land Experience or to Rosenthal's larger ministry. Not that I ever expected to have a "total sensory experience," as the ad promises, that will be educational, inspirational, etc. But I found myself repulsed. Why? Partly because I am so strongly opposed to the theological and political agendas that dominate this place, especially its apocalyptic Christian Zionism in combination with its mission to evangelize to Jewish people. And partly because I recognized in this place and its ministry a certain face of evangelical Christianity that I have come to distrust. It's the face that always inclines itself toward theological fundamentalism. It's the face that is turned on by the dream of an ideological system that is total, lock-tight, free of all logical contradiction. In this sort of theological answer machine, there is no room for doubts, uncertainties, questions.

But I think that what repelled me most about the Holy Land Experience was its lack of authenticity. I mean that in two different ways. First, it is inauthentic in that it is not forthright about its larger agendas, especially its mission to proselytize Jews into its own peculiar form of Christianity, preferring (as many understandably concerned Jews have rightly alleged) to present itself as an educational mission. Second, it was inauthentic in that the actual physical place lacked personality and soul. It was a production rather than a creation. There was no sense of creative process or personal investment in its various displays. No finger prints, no paint strokes, no mistakes, no signatures, no whimsy. The perfectly landscaped gardens around the Empty Tomb, the perfectly plumb walls of the Temple, and the expertly made costumes of the performers left me longing for the bumpy roads of Journey Trail, the blue barrels of the Dome of the Ark, and the hand-painted cutouts of biblical characters at Holy Land USA.

But the most significant difference between the Holy Land Experience and Holy Land USA is not a matter of production values—

high-tech versus homespun. Nor is it a matter of location—the Disneyfied interstate tourism industry of Orlando, Florida, versus the blue highways and Blue Ridge Mountains of Bedford County, Virginia. The most significant difference between these two biblical re-creations concerns the hospitality each one offers. One is primarily experiential whereas the other is primarily ideological. Whereas Holy Land USA intends to host a religious experience through an encounter with the biblical narrative that makes it "really real" in the present, the Holy Land Experience intends to host an induction of visitors into an ideology that links a certain historical view of ancient Israel to a certain biblical-theological anticipation of what will happen concerning Israel and Jerusalem before the Second Coming. Populated by live biblical characters who act in Broadway-style musicals, the Holy Land Experience has been created as a popular, relatively accessible entry point into Rev. Rosenthal's ideological-theological movement, Zion's Hope Inc.

After my encounter with the tourist from Arkansas in the gift-shop line, I wandered over to the Jerusalem model, where the man in the Indiana Jones getup was in the middle of his lecture on Jerusalem to a large crowd of Holy Landers seeking shelter from the storm. By this point he had moved from Jerusalem in the first century CE to Jerusalem today, and he was excitedly detailing recent indications that we are witnessing the beginning of the end of days, the restoration of the Temple, and the Second Coming of the Messiah. He held up the most recent issue of *Zion's Fire* magazine, encouraging those interested in pursuing these things in greater depth to take and read it, mentioning in particular Rev. Rosenthal's article on Iraq and the Middle East. I took and read. In that article, Rosenthal presents Iraq as the modern incarnation of ancient Babylon, enemy of God's beloved Israel. He argues that its hatred toward Israel and America is in fact satanic. Indeed, this "city of Satan" stands against Jerusalem, the city of God. What we are witnessing, Rosenthal declares, is an escalation of conflict that is moving the world closer and closer to the final apocalyptic battle between Jesus Christ, who will restore the line of King David and rule from Jerusalem, and the Antichrist, who will rule from the satanic beast empires: Iraq, which he identifies as the heir of ancient Babylon; Syria, which he identifies with ancient Greece; and Iran, which he identifies with ancient Persia. Although he hesitates to say conclusively, he suspects that the fourth satanic beast, the heir of the Roman Empire, may be the United Nations.

While standing in the lobby corner reading the magazine, longing to go back to the Jerusalem Street Market with my kids and pet some goats or have a turkey leg at the Oasis Palms Café, I overheard two older gentlemen talking in the lobby while they waited for their wives to return from the restroom.

"I tell you," one said under his breath to the other, "I just wish there was a *pill* I could take that'd make me understand all that. I mean, all those dates and signs, and all the Bible verses to back 'em up. I just can't keep it all straight."

Indeed, it appeared to me that although visitors were generally entertained and delighted by the various attractions and performances of the Holy Land Experience, most were baffled if not turned off by the prevalence of the apocalyptic theology of Zion's Hope. Like my chagrined friend from Arkansas, they were looking for a religious experience. They want to inhabit their sacred stories, recreate sacred space and time.

Like the man in the white robe sitting in the empty tomb in the Gospel of Mark, I wanted to say, "You seek Jesus of Nazareth . . . he is not here," and suggest that they try Virginia.

Chapter Three

STATIONS OF THE COURSE

Golgotha Fun Park
Cave City, Kentucky

Biblical Mini-Golf
Lexington, Kentucky

The miles of deep subterranean passageways and caverns in southern Kentucky's Mammoth Cave National Park have been a major tourist attraction since the late nineteenth century, when they were considered a must-see on what came to be known as the American Grand Tour. Tourists descending with their guides into the cold, darkly sublime underground spaces often experience something closely akin to religious awe—a feeling of creaturely smallness, of being in the belly of mystery, at once terrified and fascinated. Many feel as though they are visiting a sacred place, a natural cathedral specially designed and created by God.

With names like the Valley of Humility, The Bottomless Pit, and Bunyan's Way, moreover, the tour experience was originally intended to be something of a pilgrimage, attracting travelers with hopes of receiving some kind of divine revelation. Indeed, authors of popular early travel narratives about Mammoth Cave and other natural wonders of the American Grand Tour often described themselves and their fellow travelers as pilgrims.

Golgotha Fun Park

My family spent a day in Mammoth Caves National Park on our way from Alabama to southern Kentucky during our initial tour of roadside religious America. On our American not-so-Grand Tour, however, Mammoth Cave was a side trip. The main religious attraction for us in southern Kentucky was another sort of sacred space close by: Golgotha Fun Park, a biblically themed miniature golf course in Cave City, Kentucky, a few miles due east of Mammoth Cave National Park on Highway 70.

Loaded with hotels and RV parks, Cave City is first and foremost a place to stay while visiting the caves. But it does have its own family activities and attractions: Big Mike's Mystery House, Old Yeller Water Slide, Rock-N-Roll Bumper Boats, Alpine Slide, Cave Country Go Carts, a Wild West resort called Guntown Mountain. And then, of course, there's Golgotha Fun Park. After plumbing the depths of the sublime in the caves, who wouldn't want to putt-putt away an afternoon at Golgotha Fun Park?

Cresting Calvary Hill on Highway 70, one is more likely to experience delighted bewilderment than religious awe upon encountering the risen Christ, standing on top of the empty tomb, his head tilted warmly toward the fairway of the eighteenth hole, watching on encouragingly as golfers take in their final shot at a hole-in-one.

Self-proclaimed (and probably unchallenged) as "The World's Largest Shaded Miniature Golf Course," the eighteen holes of Golgotha Fun Park tell a biblical tale that runs from creation to Resurrection. The miniature fairway for each hole is covered in green indoor-outdoor carpet and framed with pressure-treated two-by-six boards. In the middle of the graveled property is a fairly large clubhouse with a café and video games. Concrete tables suitable for picnicking between biblical episodes are located throughout the park.

The course begins in Genesis 2, that is, with some considerable

Golgotha Fun Park, Cave City, Kentucky

stretch of imagination, in the Garden of Eden. Near the hole are two Romanesque fiberglass figures, Adam and Eve. The original couple is nude, each covering her or his private parts with something biblically telltale: a red apple for Eve and a fig leaf for Adam. The snake is coiled next to a pot as though he's lost his stereotypical turbaned, flute-playing charmer. He looks on from a distance as Eve leans toward Adam with that winning smile of hers, perhaps inviting him to try the fruit. (But how can this be? They don't become aware of their nakedness and cover their privates with leaves until after eating.) Adam is turned away from her, his eyes conveying both confusion and distrust as he strikes a pose that will one day become the trademark stance, sans leaf, of his distant and less modest descendant, King David.

The second hole is Noah's Ark, where one must putt the ball straight through a tunnel under the boat while happy gray squirrels,

Hole One: Adam and Eve, Golgotha Fun Park

beavers, bunnies (two kinds), and alligators form an orderly queue, two by two, outside. No water hazards here. Apparently this scene is still barely prediluvian.

At hole three, Jonah sits patiently, hands neatly folded across his knees, on the tongue of an open-jawed whale. Moses parts the

Red Sea for the ball to pass through at hole four. The walls of the fiberglass-sculpted sea are decorated with dangling Christmas lights, which must be spectacular during night golfing. Themes for the remaining Old Testament holes include the Ten Commandments, the Golden Calf episode, and Daniel in the lion's den.

Many of the holes could use some restoration work. Daniel needs a good scrubbing, not to mention some touch-up paint. And the lions he faces look like they've been ridden by younger putters a few too many times. The little gold-painted plaster calf lying in the corner of sixth hole seemed to be looking disgustedly at his putting green, dark with mildew and cluttered with leaves and sticks. The plywood layers of the two tablets of the Ten Commandments are separating, and the paint is so badly peeled and faded that you can't read their prohibitions to save your soul.

Just behind the Ten Commandments hole, there is a small building with a large hand-painted sign advertising an alternative amusement: PAINT BALL WAR. Commandment number six is "Thou shalt not kill," but apparently pretending with paintball is okay.

The ninth hole, a nativity scene, marks the transition to the New Testament "back nine." Everyone knows the Old Testament is more interesting for a theme park than the New—more action, more sex, more violence, more morally complex characters, more spectacular miracles (with all due respect for Jesus's healings, exorcisms, and Resurrection). Perhaps of necessity, then, the New Testament series is a little slow to begin. Once past the nativity scene, you putt your way through a series of displays that illustrate parables and other teachings of Jesus, none of which offer very clever or challenging obstacles for golfers, even if they may for lawyers, rich men, and young rulers. A little Dutch maid holds a sheep close to her bosom (the parabolic good shepherd), for example, and Jesus stands at the well where he offered a word of grace to the Samaritan woman. Mary and Martha kneel prayerfully on either side of their putting green.

"Golgotha," which is Aramaic for "the skull," and which refers in the Gospels to the place where Jesus was crucified, is the sixteenth hole. Here two ceramic skulls, painted blue with white teeth, sit on round concrete pads along the fairway. Although they don't pose much of a putting challenge, they *are* rather creepy and distracting.

Towering above the seventeenth hole are three whitewashed crosses made of four-by-four lumber, now rotting from weather exposure. Taking a sharp turn between the central cross and the one for the thief to Jesus's left, putters finally meet the risen Lord standing at the end of a relatively long fairway atop the empty tomb, a square brick structure with a single small opening. The stone is rolled away, Jesus is out. In goes the ball.

It's not easy to venture a theological interpretation of Golgotha Fun Park. Yet I am compelled to try. The eighteenth hole, the hole of Resurrection and salvation, appears to be the easiest one to make. Perhaps that's by design. The real obstacles come before, in the events leading to the Crucifixion, the death of the beloved son. Indeed, as Paul says, it is the scandal of the Cross, the belief in a crucified God, which is a great stumbling block to faith. The darkness of Good Friday comes before the sunrise of Easter Sunday. A good miniature golf course needs good obstacles—challenging but surmountable for parents and kids alike. The putting obstacles in Golgotha Fun Park are, we might say, both athletic and theological.

For most of us, of course, it's not the course's outstandingly challenging or clever holes that draw us to this place. It's the name. "Golgotha," "the place of the skull," doesn't exactly go with "fun." Whether intentional or not, the jarring association of skulls, Crucifixion, and fun is a stroke of poetic genius uncommon in the world of miniature golf, let alone theology. Not that "Calvary" is any less peppy in biblical terms. In fact, "calvary" is simply the Latin transla-tion in the Vulgate New Testament for the Aramaic term "golgotha" (Matthew 27: "...*Golgotha quod est Calvariae locus,*" "Golgotha which is the place of the Skull"). Both words mean "skull," and both refer in the Gospels to the place of Jesus's execution. Yet, some-how, in popular American Christian culture, "calvary" is far more mainstream and palatable. It's used everywhere: Calvary Fellow-ship, Calvary Chapel, Calvary Park, Camp Calvary. "Golgotha" has maintained its deathly skullish overtones, but Calvary has largely left them behind. Calvary Fun Park would raise few eyebrows.

But this fun park has opted for the less expected and more jarring. "Golgotha" and "fun park" create cognitive dissonance, combining lighthearted attraction with mortality and the death of God. They cause a category jam.

With Golgotha Fun Park, I have to wonder if the horror and re-pulsion won out over the shiny happy fun. Shocking and disappoint-ing as it may be to some, the course is closed, with no indication that it will re-open in the near future. By the time my family and I had ar-rived to take our swings at parting the Red Sea, no one was there to rent us balls and putters. It was a green-carpeted biblical ghost town. Despite the eighteenth hole's glorious proclamation to the contrary, it looks as though death, not Resurrection, has won out at Golgotha Fun Park. At least for the time being.

Fortunately for us, Golgotha isn't the only biblical fun park in the area. Another is but a few hours' drive away.

Fifty-Four Holes to Glory

The three eighteen-hole courses of biblical miniature golf at the family-owned and operated Lexington Ice Center & Sports Complex are open, and business appears to be booming. As we parked our motor home in the huge parking lot, we quickly realized why Golgotha Fun Park had to qualify itself as the world's largest *shaded* golf course. For this sprawling, absolutely shadeless acre or so of artificial turf sporting brightly colored biblical obstacles is several times larger than its Cave City competitor. Its clubhouse is clean and orderly, with a friendly staff to set you up with the right putter, a scorecard, and a printed guide that explains the biblical significance of each hole. Clearly this place is topflight.

Tom and Sally Christopher began building the courses soon after purchasing the ice rink and its surrounding property in 1985. Devout Christians, the Christophers believe that God led them to this project, which they consider to be a public ministry, that is, a fun way for people, especially youth, to learn biblical stories and verses. It was also a wise business move: every spring, as interest in ice skating decreases, interest in miniature golf increases.

Nearly two decades since their opening, these well-maintained courses continue to be a popular pastime for locals—especially church youth groups, to whom the Christophers regularly send ad materials. It also attracts miniature-golf enthusiasts who travel the country in search of unique courses (yes, such people do exist).

Each of the three courses has its own biblical theme: the first is the Old Testament, the second is the New Testament, and the third is Miracles. Each hole on each course centers on a single biblical passage, which is displayed at the tee-off point along with par for the course. No matter where you tee off, you're within earshot of the Christian music piped across the greens from the clubhouse.

The Old Testament course is very Genesis-heavy. The first seven holes are dedicated to the seven days of creation, culminating with God's Shabbat on the seventh (a par three, as I recall). The eighth hole, the Garden of Eden, has as its focal point a nicely rounded maple representing the prohibited tree of the knowledge of good and evil. There's no Eve or Adam or serpent in sight. This is certainly an ambiguous obstacle. Does sinking it mean you have escaped temptation, or that you have succumbed to it and are now ready to leave the Garden? After all, that's the only way to get on with the rest of the story.

After leaving Paradise, golfers go straight to cosmic destruction as they putt through the middle of a large Noah's Ark at the ninth hole. The post-Flood rainbow is number ten. Consistent with Sunday-school versions, the biblical passages at the tees of these two holes, Genesis 7:1–24 and 9:8–17, avoid the most horrific and theologically problematic aspects of this story, namely God's determination that all humanity is rotten to the core, the mass annihilation that ensues, and God's subsequent regret.

After the Flood, the narrative pace picks up considerably as putters quickly skim through the rest of the Old Testament: up Jacob's ladder; through the plagues of Egypt (represented by three cute frogs surrounding hole twelve), into the volcano-like top of Mount. Sinai, through conquered Jericho, along the blade of Delilah's scissors, out the handle of David's slingshot, and finally, after a brief mini-meditation on the Twenty-third Psalm ("The Lord is my shepherd..."), in and out of the whale that swallowed Jonah.

In Christian tradition, Jonah, who remained in the whale for three days and three nights before he was spit out on the shores of Ninevah, is interpreted to be a precursor of Jesus, who was resurrected on the third day. As the eighteenth and final hole on the first course, then, Jonah anticipates the second course, the theme of which is the New Testament. This course, too, follows a biblical narrative, although more loosely presented. After the first hole, the star of Bethlehem, we might expect the second to be a manger scene. But no. The course jumps immediately from Matthew 1 to the Acts of the Apostles: hole two is Damascus Road, on which Saul, soon to become the Apostle Paul, was temporarily blinded and stopped from persecuting followers of Jesus. The third, Jailhouse Rock, is about the imprisonment of Paul and his companion Silas. From there, the course returns to a series of holes with themes drawn from various teachings of the Gospels and letters. The three final holes recite the three gifts of the spirit named by Paul in his first letter to the church at Corinth: "faith, hope, and love . . . and the greatest of these is love." The eighteenth hole, then, is Love in Any Language, a par two with a long straight fairway. Above the hole is a small case displaying a hanging globe, Bibles in various languages, Barbie dolls in national costumes, and a figure-skater Ken doll wearing a purple cape.

The third course focuses on biblical miracle stories, from Moses's burning bush (my personal favorite—a knee-high wood-framed box with a light inside, wrapped in purple and green plastic vines), to Elisha's floating axe head, to Jesus feeding the five thousand, to the Resurrection. There are two holes with carpets that transition from blue to red: the fifth, representing the Exodus plague in which the water was turned to blood; and the eleventh, representing Jesus's first miracle, when he turned water into wine during the wedding celebration at Cana. The two should not be confused.

The ninth hole in the Miracle course, called "He's Alive!," is a Calvary display similar to those we've seen at other biblical recreation sites: three empty crosses on a raised stone structure with an empty tomb down below. This is not only the middle of the third course but also the center and focal point of the entire property, visible from any point on any course. Spatially, then, this theological pairing of death and Resurrection is the orientation point, the axis mundi, the center of this entire world of biblical narrative. Whereas the courses themselves are experienced diachronically ("through-time"), moving golfers through episodes of the Christian biblical narrative as they move from one hole to the next, this Calvary display organizes the experience in a synchronic way, so that all the different narrative episodes are given their ultimate meaning in relation to a single point in space and time, that of the Crucifixion and Resurrection. It is the point that orients and coordinates all other points.

Burning Bush, Lexington Ice Center & Sports Complex

Holy Pastime

Religion is riddled with paradoxes, and Christianity is no exception: dying to the self in order to live...wisdom that is folly in the eyes of the world...power through surrender...in the world but not of it...the first shall be last...three in one...fully God and fully human. Above all, there is what scholars call the paradox of the sacred, that is, the fact that the sacred, the "wholly other," that which is radically other and beyond reason or imagination to conceive or represent, is revealed in and through the profane, the ordinary, the everyday. This is the paradox. There is no experience of the sacred outside the profane. The sacred, which is radically other than the profane, is revealed in and through the profane. A rock in a riverbed becomes a sacred embodiment of the divine. A natural spring becomes a source of holy water. A loaf of bread becomes the body of Christ. A streak of detergent on the window of a downtown building becomes a revelation of the Blessed Virgin Mary. Radical otherness is revealed in and through sameness, the extraordinary through the ordinary, the transcendent through the immanent.

Biblical minigolf has to be one of the most remarkable illustrations of this fundamental paradox of the sacred in American leisure culture. We might call it a *holy pastime*. In biblical minigolf, sacred scripture is made incarnate in a trivial pursuit.

And miniature golf is America's quintessential trivial pursuit. Granted there was some utility in its early predecessors—private courses laid out in backyards and on city rooftops designed for putting practice. The earliest of these is commonly held to be the eighteen-hole, carefully landscaped "Thistle Dhu" course in North Carolina, built for James Barber in 1916 as a miniature replica of a full-size golf course. By the 1930s, however, miniature golf had exploded into a pastime of its own, losing all connection to the more serious sport of golf. According to miniature golf historian Susan R.

Chandler, author of "Lilli-putt-ian Landmarks: History and Significance of Miniature Golf Courses," we owe this transformation especially to Frieda and Garnet Carter, who in 1926 created their whimsical Tom Thumb course, complete with underground pipeways, gnomes, and Little Red Riding Hood, in the front yard of their inn on Lookout Mountain on the Tennessee-Georgia border. Soon the Carters were manufacturing and selling Tom Thumb golf courses throughout the United States. Other franchisers followed, as did many mom-and-pop entrepreneurs with their own peculiar visions of artificial turfscapes.

But nothing stands still in today's competitive miniature golf market. To keep renting out putters and balls you need more than boilerplate courses with gnomes, loop-di-loops, and bottomless eighteenth holes. You need a coherent theme. Not just any coherent theme but one that transforms the course into a thematically coherent miniature world, a fantasy world—a pirate treasure hunt or an African safari, to cite the two most common examples. Miniature golf aficionados distinguish such courses by calling them "Adventure Golf."

As the term "Adventure Golf" implies, these courses give the space of the course a narrative form. They are miniature story worlds. Following the path from the first to the eighteenth hole, putters move through a story. There is only one way through the space. (Don't you feel sneaky on a miniature golf course when you skip a couple holes, or go back and do one again at the end? Perhaps that's because you're breaking the narrative rules of the course.) Each hole is part of a larger thematically coherent story world that provides the context for the total mini-golf experience.

Given the century-old American tradition of re-creating "the world of the Bible" in small-scale form, the invention of biblical miniature golf was probably inevitable. (The two we've explored here, by the way, are not the only ones. I hear there's one in Denver, Colorado, at the Noah's Ark Park, and another in Du Quoin, Illinois. There are probably others as well.)

Like their more serious biblically recreative predecessors, these courses are Christian story worlds based on a certain recounting of biblical narrative. They put biblical narrative into spatial form, stringing episodes together into a story that moves from creation to fall to redemption. They put pilgrims on a story-line from Genesis to Resurrection. The ultimate goal is evangelistic, a revelation of the truth of the Gospel that will lead to life-transforming personal conversion or reformation and ultimately, their creators hope, to Revelation. The nineteenth hole, we might say, is the altar call.

With biblical minigolf, then, sacred narrative, The Greatest Story Ever Told, meets one of the most trivial of all American amusements. Here biblical narrative is reduced to a series of green-carpeted putting greens with Noah instead of Tom Thumb, a burning bush instead of a windmill, and an empty tomb instead of a bottomless hole. Putting one's way from hole to hole through sacred narrative, one finds the ultimate trivial pursuit converging with ultimate meaning. In this concentrated form of religious pastime, then, we witness a simultaneous trivialization of the sacred and consecration of the trivial.

Distinguishing itself from the formalities of well-established higher church denominations, American evangelical Christianity, especially its youth culture, has tended to play fast and loose with its more formal heritage. This is the movement that brought us electric-guitar accompaniment for hymns, Oreo-and-milk Communion services, and birthday cakes for baby Jesus on Christmas. What motivates such footloose and fancy-free alterations and adaptations of traditional religious practice to pop culture is above all the desire to reach otherwise uninterested non-Christians with the Gospel message. Such practices pique interest by shaking up expectations and stereotypes of what it means to be Christian. You thought Christians were stuffy, moralistic, uptight, but look how wild and crazy we can be! The aim is to make it appealingly fun.

But what makes such practices seem so fun, especially to youth? I suggest it's the element of transgression built into them. They are social activities that transgress the boundaries of expected religious practice and behavior in something of a carnivalesque fashion. They might even be called sacrilegious, in that they violate established rules and patterns of behavior in relation to sacred things and sacred rites. Often the transgression is not a conscious act. Think of young kids playing after a church worship service in the altar space, where the priests had been officiating sacred rites only minutes before. They know, even if not consciously, from the behavior of parents and clergy during worship that the space is set apart as "sacred," and that their play in that space transgresses the boundaries that mark and maintain its sacredness. Often evangelical playfulness with tradition is similarly subconscious.

Biblical mini-golf, as a trivialization of sacred scripture, is another instance of this kind of playful transgression. It opens up something of a carnival space within biblical literature. Sacred stories from a sacred book normally read and discussed in the context of worship or devotional study here become silly obstacles in a superficial pastime. No doubt this accounts for its popularity among youth groups. Biblical mini-golf makes biblical narrative into carnival space. It literally makes fun of sacred scripture. But with biblical mini-golf, the religious dimensions of the experience are quickly overcome by the trivial challenges of the play.

While I talked with the staff in the clubhouse and took pictures of the courses at Lexington Ice Center & Sports Complex, my family played through all fifty-four holes. Trying for the full biblical

mini-golf experience, Clover insisted that the kids guess what biblical episode or theme each hole represented and then read the plaque
at the tee to check their answers. Their Sunday school teachers
might be pleased to know that their biblical literacy scores were
pretty good. But they were far more interested in their golf scores.
The biblical dimensions of the courses were far less compelling than
their putting challenges. They noted in passing what they'd almost
come to expect by that point on our road trip. "Hey, Dad, look over
there," Seth yelled past the Tree of Life from the volcanic-looking
Mount Sinai, "another empty tomb with crosses on top. You should
go look at it." But then it was back to the more compelling attraction: catching up to his sister, who had gotten ahead of him thanks
to a very impressive under-par performance at the plague of frogs.

Indeed, despite its prominence on the property, and despite its
religious significance, and despite the obvious investment of time
and labor creating it, the "He's Alive" ninth hole, Calvary and
empty tomb, wasn't very interesting as a golfing challenge. In fact,
my kids ended up skipping it and going back to Exodus to replay
Mount Sinai. In Christian narrative terms, that's something like
turning your back on the New Law of the Gospel and returning to
the Old Law.

Of course, as was the case at Golgotha Fun Park, making the
empty tomb a greater challenge might have posed theological prob-
lems for the evangelical creators of this course, since it might have
given some players negative associations with what they would
consider to be the centerpiece of Christian faith. And they wouldn't
want people hurling their putters at the Cross in a rage. Better, they
perhaps speculated, to err in the other direction, allowing more biblically peripheral episodes to offer the greatest challenges for players.

Ultimately, then, it may be that biblical mini-golf simply cannot
maintain the paradox of the sacred. As the superficial overcomes the

deep, the sacred cannot inhere in the profane. The profane amusement and distraction of the play overcomes the narrative experience, leaving putters not at the foot of the Cross but returning to Mount Sinai, struggling not to make that ultimate leap of faith but rather to get just the right speed on the ball to make it up that slope without going over the top.

The dilemma of biblical mini-golf is this: how to have fun with holy scripture without forfeiting its status as sacred text, the Word of God. Is this not also the dilemma of evangelical Christianity more generally, especially within its youth culture? Although we tend to think of American evangelical Christianity as a conservative movement (focusing on its positions concerning sexuality, reproductive rights, drugs and alcohol, and matters of biblical authority), in fact it tends to be the most liberal of Christianities when it comes to its appropriating and adapting tradition to the popular interests and consumer demands of the secular mainstream. In this, the dilemma is the same: how to maintain the sacred in the profane. What keeps it from becoming a complete carnivalization of tradition? Does it ultimately sacrifice the sacred, so to speak, in the name of spreading its Gospel?

Chapter Four

NOWADAY NOAH

God's Ark of Safety
Frostburg, Maryland

NOAH'S ARK BEING REBUILT HERE!

Without this sign planted prominently on the mountainside near Frostburg, few if any passersby on Interstate 68 would recognize the forty-five-foot-high reddish brown girder framework resting and rusting there as any sort of boat-in-progress. Indeed, what on first impression makes little *business* sense as a multilevel parking garage or office building (location, location, location) makes even less initial *religious* sense as a Noah's Ark rebuilding project.

But for a veteran Sunday school kid like me, the fact that this is a Noah's Ark presents a particular challenge. If you know the story the way most Sunday school kids do, then you know that just by seeing an Ark-in-progress like this, you've become part of its Noah's story. Granted, the biblical account in Genesis doesn't have much to say about Noah's neighbors and passersby. God declares them to be irredeemably wicked and decides to wipe them out and save the household of Noah, who is "righteous in his generation." (What if he'd lived in another generation? Never mind, children.) They don't talk to Noah. If you were to make a Noah movie that sticks strictly to the details of the biblical account, you wouldn't even need to hire extras for the crowds. They're practically not there. They're declared wicked, and then they're gone.

But Sunday school teachers have long recognized the potential for instilling the fear of God in kids by giving Noah's neighbors and passersby a more significant role to play in the story. Perhaps picking up on the fact that God pronounces them all rotten through and through, Sunday school retellings of the story on flannel boards and in coloring books invariably present them as Noah's ruthless hecklers. They chide. They taunt. They laugh at crazy Noah as he builds an absurdly large boat in his backyard. Which I suppose makes some kids feel better when the rain begins to fall and they all get drowned in torrents of divine wrath. But it also makes every kid who sees them laughing away on the flannel board think, "Gosh, I hope *I* wouldn't be like *those* people."

So for a church kid like me, a Noah's Ark-in-progress on the side of the road presents something of a dilemma. As soon as it catches your eye, the Noah who's building it has roped you into his story. Like it or not, know it or not, you've got a part to play. If you ignore his Ark project, then you're no better than the best of the unrighteous masses that ignored Noah until they were in over their heads. And if you laugh or even scoff, then you're no better than the worst. Either way, as far as this Noah is concerned, you're among those who won't know till it's too late. As the water begins to rise, he imagines, he'll be hearing your cries over the barks and brays of his little in-houseboat zoo. *Now* who's the fool? You're caught in his sense of irony. And that pushes a church kid's buttons.

Travelers seeking more than a drive-by chuckle, or who are fool enough not to want to be this Noah's fool, need to take the Frostburg exit just east of the Ark and loop around the back side on Cherry Lane. From the highway, all you see is the steel framework of the

View from the Parking Lot, God's Ark of Safety

Ark's bow. From the parking lot behind it, however, you have a fuller view of the Ark's huge foundation system, which provides a much better impression of the intended total size. The structure visible from the highway, in fact, is only the first phase of the larger project—the front third. The foundation, poured from over three thousand tons of concrete, is one-and-a-half football fields long. Each of its more than seventy footers is sunk sixteen feet into the ground. This is to accommodate an Ark built to biblical specifications, for size if not for building materials—three hundred cubits long, fifty cubits wide, and thirty cubits high, according to the Almighty's blueprint in Genesis 6. In lay terms, that translates to approximately four-hundred-and-fifty by seventy-five by forty-five feet (assuming a cubit is about eighteen inches). It's a project of mythological proportions, literally.

When I visited, the grass in and around the foundation area had been freshly mown. A backhoe was parked at one end, as if a work crew were off on a lunch break. But it was ten in the morning—too early for lunch break—and there was no crew. It was as though I had come upon a work in progress without progress. It reminded me of one of those scenes from left-behind type movies in which everyone had been taken up in the rapture, leaving all their projects unfinished.

Next to the Ark is a long rectangular beige aluminum building with "God's Ark of Safety Ministries" and a rainbow painted on the parking lot end. The side door opens onto a chapel space, with seating for about a hundred and fifty. On the wall behind the pulpit is a large mural painting of Jesus, floating in the sky and gesturing with open hands toward a cross that emanates rays of white light.

Toward the rear of the chapel is a reception area and office space, which serves as the base of operations for Richard Greene, founder, pastor, and head of God's Ark of Safety and the Noachic visionary behind this Ark-in-progress.

A friendly, soft-spoken, tucked-in gentleman in his sixties, Pastor Greene greeted me warmly and escorted me back to his office. There were lots of rainbows and Ark-related images decorating the room, but what initially grabbed my attention was a painting leaning against the wall near his desk. It was a close-up image of Jesus's face, almost photographic in style. He was on the Cross, crowned in thorns, blood and sweat dripping down his face, but was looking directly at his viewers with a warm, reassuring smile, as if to say, "It's okay! Everything's going according to plan!"

Noticing my disturbed fascination with this image, Pastor Greene explained. "An artist friend did that for our ministry. We're selling signed copies and all the proceeds are going to building the Ark!"

I was beginning to realize that everything but everything here re-lated somehow to the Ark project. This was a man single-mindedly pursuing a vision.

"So tell me about the Ark," I followed. "How did it get started?" And with that question, the floodgates were opened. For the next couple hours, without so much as an interruption from me or the phone, Pastor Greene told me his story, highs and lows, hopes and fears.

The Vision

It all started back in the spring of 1974, shortly after moving from Pontiac, Michigan, to Frostburg with his wife, Lottie, and younger daughter to serve as part-time minister in a small Church of the Brethren congregation. His other job was as a nurse in the local hospital.

Not long after arriving and settling in, he began having night visions. Every night for three months in a row, his sleep was inter-rupted by the same two-part dream, which he describes as though it were a movie.

The first part of the vision was set in the biblical story world. He would see Noah working diligently on his Ark while nearby crowds of people mocked and laughed at him (clearly he'd had the same Sunday school curriculum as I'd had). Pastor Greene felt as though he were right there next to Noah—"as plain as my hands before my eyes." Occasionally Noah would turn to the chiding crowds and preach, pleading with them to turn from their sins and come to God before it was too late. Then Pastor Greene saw the rain begin to fall and the waters begin to rise. Noah's mockers screamed and ran to-ward the Ark. But God had shut the door. The first part of the vision ended with the Ark floating on a vast glassy sea with no other signs of life.

Then came a second, contemporary scene in which Pastor Greene was standing on a stage area in front of a large audience inside a high-tech, modern-day Noah's Ark.

"The theater was one of those IMAX types, and on the big huge screen was a movie showing the biblical Noah's Ark story exactly as I had seen it in the first part of my dream vision. And then the movie would cut to present-day world events—floods, famines, wars, hurricanes."

Interspersed with these images of disaster, as a kind of biblical commentary, he and his audience saw prophetic sayings from the Bible describing (as Greene understood them) what will occur during the final days before divine judgment—floods, famines, wars, and hurricanes, of course. "And then, at the end of the film, I saw people getting up from their seats and coming forward to accept Jesus."

The implication was that the film within the dream was actually made or at least directed by God. "You see, God was showing me that he wanted me to rebuild the Ark, and that he'd use film to reveal the signs of the coming judgment and to call people to repent and receive him."

Ironically interpolating a little Tower of Babel into his vision of Noah's Ark, Greene said he saw people coming to the Ark from all corners of the world, speaking many different languages. He saw a parking lot full of cars and motor homes and tour buses. The Ark, he believed, would serve as a warning to repent before it's too late, before the figurative and literal waters begin to rise once again.

For a long time he didn't share this vision with anyone, even Lottie. He feared being made a laughingstock by his new parishioners and neighbors. But the dreams kept tormenting him. He asked God for a sign to confirm what he feared, that he should present his vision of a re-created Noah's Ark to his small church congregation as a new building campaign. Not long after, while browsing a local bookstore, he stumbled upon a book about the Noah's Ark in which were pictures of what it might have looked like.

"As I looked at the pictures, I realized they were *exactly like* the Ark in my dreams! My heart began to thump hard. It was like electricity was coursing through my body. My knees got weak like jelly, and I had to lean against a wall to keep from falling to the ground." He stumbled home and gave himself over to what he now believed was God's will for him, to rebuild Noah's Ark as a warning to all people to repent before the hard rains begin to fall.

In our conversation, Pastor Greene recounted the next three decades of the rebuilding project, still very much in progress, as a series of signs and miracles. He worried about how to present the vision to his congregation until a stranger, who turned out to be an architect, turned up at his door and offered to do the initial drawings and plans. While driving to a convention of ministers, he asked God for a sign as to whether he should share the vision there, and immediately saw the word *ARK* clearly legible on the mud flap of the truck in front of him (it actually said *CLARK*, but God had apparently blotted out the *CL* with mud). When they needed to rent a bulldozer to level the foundation area, a businessman—named Mr. Hope—loaned five of them to use. A 1975 interview on *The 700 Club*, an evangelical Christian television show, led to a burst of international media attention that brought in a new stream of funding. Lo and behold, moreover, the other guest on that same *700 Club* show was the author of the Noah's Ark book that had jellied his knees the previous year.

And then there are the healings. Since he received his vision, he believes, God has given him the gift of healing. It began with the near death of an elderly woman in his church, after which his fame began to spread throughout the Frostburg area. "Backs...I heal hundreds of backs." Once, he claimed, he healed a whole hospital full of patients. "The next day I came back and all the rooms were empty!" He even "healed" one of the cardio machines there ("I smiled at the nurses, put my hand on the machine, and said, 'Machine, be healed!' And the next day they were amazed when it worked again!"). For Greene, these healings, too, are signs that point people to the Ark. They legitimate him and his project.

The land itself, he claimed, has healing powers. People have sometimes been healed of chronic illnesses simply by setting foot on the property. One volunteer builder, for example, was healed of a lifelong sun allergy. On his second day working there, he realized he no longer needed a hat and long sleeves to protect his skin from sun exposure. As with miraculous healing stories associated with grottos and other traditional pilgrimage destinations, such stories about this land's healing powers have at least two effects. First, they sanctify the place, that is, they consecrate the land itself, setting it apart as holy ground. Second, they identify it as a locus of healing and blessing, that is, a place where one might reconsecrate oneself. In both ways, they draw people to the site to learn about the project and offer support.

Greene told many other stories, all confirming his sense of calling to this project as a holy work. Indeed, as Greene told his story to me, it seemed that rarely a week had gone by without another miraculous sign that God was still at work.

Someone else might tell a very different story, one that another believer in divine signs might take to mean that this Ark project is dead in the water. As he gives his own positive testimony, Pastor Greene alludes to potential episodes in such a counterstory often enough to get a sense of how it would go. It'd be a story of numerous stalls in construction, alienation from the community leadership of the town of Frostburg, a split with his denomination and many former parishioners, accusations of financial mismanagement, and confrontations with other local ministers who feel he needs to let the project go. Indeed, some of those who were enthusiastic supporters during the early years have turned on him more recently, asking whether all the delays ought to be taken as divine interventions intended to make Pastor Greene abandon the project.

How does he face such confrontations and counterclaims? He arms himself with biblical assurances: "Blessed are they which are persecuted for righteousness' sake" (Matthew 5:10). And remember "when once the longsuffering of God waited in the days of Noah, while the Ark was a preparing" in order to save but one family (1 Peter 3:20).

WWND? (What Would Noah Do?)

As Pastor Greene's story makes particularly clear, biblical recreation is sometimes not just a matter of re-creating particular places or scenarios from the Bible. It may also be about re-creating *oneself* in biblical terms. Noah's Ark is being rebuilt here, but Noah himself is also in some sense being reincarnated here. Or rather, Pastor Greene is remaking himself in Noah's image. In the long course of this Ark project, Pastor Greene has come to see his life as a contemporary reenactment of the biblical Noah story.

In some ways, the literary craft of the biblical Noah story invites lifelong reenactments like Pastor Greene's. As elsewhere in Genesis and the Torah, the evocative literary power of this biblical text is an effect of its strict economy of words and profound lack of detail. In an essay called "Odysseus' Scar," Erich Auerbach famously illustrated this feature of biblical narrative by contrasting the remarkably brief yet theologically freighted story of the Akeda, or "binding" of Abraham's son Isaac in Genesis 22, against the moment in Homer's *Odyssey* when Odysseus's nurse Euryclea recognizes him after touching a childhood scar while washing his feet. As she feels the scar, the story of how he got it comes to her, and is recounted in great detail as a long flashback. As this story unfolds, everything is externalized. Nothing is left hidden. All the background is given in full. In the paragraph-long biblical narrative of the Akeda, by contrast, nothing is made manifest. There, Auerbach writes, speech only "serves to indicate thoughts that remain unexpressed." Only those narrative elements necessary to move the narrative forward are given. Everything else is "left in obscurity." Readers are left with a story "fraught with background."

The same may be said of the Noah narrative. Despite its more complicated composition history, involving the editing together of at least two different literary strands, this narrative is extremely sparse and riddled with narrative gaps. There is no description of the boat except its overall size and a passing reference to its single portal (which God closes). There is no account of the duration of the building project or of its cargo of animals. There is no physical description of Noah or any other character, and there are no windows onto his inner thoughts or feelings. As mentioned earlier, no neighbors are noted, and there is no mention of the reactions of others to Noah, his religiosity, or his building project. There is no description of the violent deaths of those not on board the Ark, nor of the postdiluvian aftermath. Such details are "left in obscurity," and we are left with a story "fraught with background," not to mention fraught with theological questions that rival even those of the binding of Isaac.

But it is precisely this story's gaps, its lack of all but the most ele-

mental details, its being "fraught with background," that invite readers into its narrative world. It allows a reader like Pastor Greene to
find himself in it, to make its world his world and vice versa. In the
absence of narrative details, a reader like Pastor Greene supplies his
own details and background. The story isn't ultimately left to obscurity. Rather it comes to be illustrated with his very life story. The
story doesn't remain fraught with mysterious background. Rather his
story becomes its background. Pastor Greene's own life has become,
in a sense, a reenactment of the mythic time and place of Noah. It
has become the primary text by which Pastor Greene interprets and
justifies his own life-work. The ridicule he has received from former
parishioners, from townspeople and leaders of Frostburg, and from
news writers and passersby only reinforce his Noachic identity and
affirm that he's doing God's work.

For Pastor Greene, the biblical story and his own story have
merged into one single, coherent narrative, a narrative that gives
meaning and purpose to his life. In fact, before he began having the
night visions back in 1974, he had been in something of an identity
crisis. Having quit his job with General Motors in Detroit a few
years earlier, he was discouraged by others from fulfilling his sense
of call to be a missionary overseas, even after receiving his nursing
degree in order to do so. Although he was finding some success as a
minister, it was still necessary for him to work part-time as a nurse in
order to pay the bills. I suspect that this project will continue as long
as he does.

For Pastor Greene, everything that has happened is part of the
divine plan to rebuild the Ark. That includes, he let me know, my
visit with him. He told me about how others had interviewed him
and written about him, sometimes negatively. "God told me, 'Just
love 'em, I'll take care of the rest.'" He then told me solemnly that
some who had challenged or misrepresented him had been, well,

taken care of by God—"even right to death." One man fell off a ladder after publicly confronting him in the church. On his deathbed he repented of his criticism. Another critic became fatally ill and had to move to Florida.

Once again I felt those Sunday school anxieties coming back to haunt me. As I drove away, thinking about what I would write about this Ark and its nowaday Noah—he was so fascinating and so disturbing in his self-assurance, like the charismatic preacher-healer played Robert Duvall in *The Apostle*—I imagined a semitrailer barreling up behind me and smashing my minivan to bits. A preemptive divine strike.

Yet, while skeptical, I was also deeply compelled by his relentless faith in his original vision and his tireless drive to see it fulfilled. I felt no urge to point and laugh. Nor do I now. Indeed, something about this man and his story makes me lament my own dogged cynicism, lack of faith, and inability to hope for an absurd miracle.

The night before our visit, my dad called to tell me that he had been diagnosed with amyotrophic lateral sclerosis (ALS), often called Lou Gehrig's disease, a fatal motor neuron disease which attacks nerves in the spinal cord and the brain, ultimately leaving its victims unable to move a muscle, even to swallow or breathe. The phone call ended with both me and my dad sobbing, unable to say goodbye before hanging up. That was the first time, but not the last, that I'd hear my dad cry. I felt that I had been broken loose from my own past and was stumbling, sometimes free-falling, into an abysmal unknown future. That next morning, as I listened to Pastor Greene tell his story, I found it hard to concentrate, until he began talking about his healing powers. I found myself vulnerable to his charismatic confidence.

At a few points, I almost asked him to pray for my dad. Why didn't I? The most obvious reason is that I lacked faith in him and his vision. But perhaps another reason was that to ask for prayer from him, whether or not it could bring healing, would have meant entering into relationship with him on a very different level, one in which I would need to expose myself, make myself vulnerable.

I didn't go there. I remained invulnerable because I didn't want to enter into a real relationship with him. Perhaps in some sense I feared getting too close. Yes. But I also remained invulnerable for fear of making any kind of leap of faith, even a somewhat haphazard, playful, "what the hell" sort of leap. I mean, really, what could it have hurt?

Faith requires one to go further than trust allows. This is true of religious faith as much as it is of the kind of faith required of us to be in relationship with other people. Faith requires self-imperiling vulnerability. In faith, I open myself to another, to otherness, even to the wholly other. I expose myself, lay myself bare, express desire, show wounds. In this vulnerable expression of lack, fear, need, brokenness, I open myself to the unexpected—to healing, transformation, a word of grace. I leap, arms wide open, teary-eyed face and soft belly exposed, into an unknown possibility, without assurance that my leap will land me safely on solid ground. Faith requires vulnerability, desperate vulnerability.

That day, as my dad's scared, raspy, crying voice echoed in my sleep-deprived head, I felt desperate. Things were falling apart. I feared my dad's death. But more than that, I feared his fear, which I had never known in him before that phone call. Fear of death, but also fear of weakness. I would see and hear that many more times over the next sixteen months, and I would see it open him up to a kind of desperately vulnerable faith. A strength found in weakness, as the Apostle Paul puts it.

Within Christian tradition, one of the truest marks of ministers of the Gospel is a Jesus-like radical openness to the desperation of others. I see it in Clover, who possesses this amazing, shaman-like desire to help others give voice to their deepest pain and fear, and to their most desperate desires for healing and wholeness. I see this power, this charisma, in other friends who are ministers, priests, rabbis, and imams as well.

And I saw it in Pastor Greene. Wildly self-assured, Pastor Greene is also wildly vulnerable. His heart is on his sleeve. He is raw, open-faced. He is a man of faith in all its divine madness, ready and willing to expose himself prayerfully to the desperate desires, fears, and busted-open lives of others. No doubt Pastor Greene would have welcomed my story, and would have immediately gotten down on his knees and prayed. But in the end, like Noah's neighbors on the Sunday school flannel graphs, I passed.

Chapter Five

THE WORLD'S LARGEST
TEN COMMANDMENTS

Fields of the Wood
Murphy, North Carolina

These days the thousands of white water rafters, motor-homers, and gamblers filling the rivers, campgrounds, and casinos of Cherokee County, North Carolina in the Smoky Mountains of Nantahala National Forest are enough to make you forget this region's rich and often painful history. For centuries it was heartland for the Cherokee Nation, whose peoples thrived in great numbers near the waters of the Hiwassee and Tuckasegee rivers. But in the late 1830s, the United States Army built Fort Butler there as a headquarters for some 7,000 troops sent by President Andrew Jackson to carry out the Great Removal of the Cherokees to Oklahoma along the infamous Trail of Tears.

Sixty years after the Great Removal, the same region experienced a Great Awakening of the Holy Ghost, known as the Christian holiness movement, initiated around 1895 by a radical reformer named Benjamin Harding Irwin. As with the Pentecostal movement which had its start around the same time with the famous Azusa Street Revivals in Los Angeles, Irwin and other adherents of this new movement proclaimed that one's conversion to Christianity and baptism by water must be followed by a second baptism, a "baptism by fire" performed by the Holy Spirit and manifest in spiritual gifts, above all the gift of tongues. They also believed in the total sanctification of Christians through the ongoing work of the Holy Spirit. For this movement, conversion is only the beginning, and leads ultimately to one's complete spiritual purification and perfection. The holiness movement quickly took hold among Christians who had become dissatisfied with the creedal orientation of their denominations, and the holiness revival had begun.

Mainstream church communities and leaders in this predominantly Baptist and Methodist region of North Carolina and Tennessee did not respond positively to the new movement. Meetinghouses were burned. Proponents of holiness doctrine and practice were disfellowshipped and even horsewhipped. Yet, despite these persecutions and other pastoral prohibitions and condemnations, the movement continued to grow. By the turn of the century, a new leader had arisen in the Holiness Church at Camp Creek, near the Tennessee/North Carolina border: Ambrose Jessup Tomlinson (1865–1943).

Under the influence of other local ministers, this former Quaker Sunday school superintendent came to believe that the radical holiness movement sweeping the region was in fact a reawakening of the New Testament Apostolic church, a sign that Jesus would be returning very soon. In 1906, a few years after becoming head of the Camp Creek congregation, he called together a number of revivalist congregations and their ministers from Tennessee, North Carolina, and Georgia to form a new denomination. In 1907 the members approved Tomlinson's proposal to call themselves "the Church of God" (and he did mean *the* Church of God), and in 1909 Tomlinson was appointed its first General Overseer. In 1923, with church membership in the tens of thousands, Tomlinson was deposed by other leaders within the Church of God on account of financial mismanagement and his unwillingness to share power. He took two thousand loyal followers with him and formed what eventually came to be known as the Church of God of Prophecy. He remained General Overseer until his death in 1943, after which his son, Milton, led the church until his death in 1995. Today, the Church of God of Prophecy claims to have over five hundred thousand members.

The strong conviction that this new church was *the* Church of God—the reawakening of the original "New Testament church" of Jesus's first Apostles—led to a practice of biblical interpretation that saw literal fulfillments of particular passages from scripture everywhere. Central here was the doctrine of *visible signs*, that is, the belief that the various events of the time were literal, visible fulfillments of specific biblical passages. In the biblical book of Habakkuk, God tells the prophet, "Write the vision, ... for the vision is yet for an appointed time, *but at the end it shall speak.*" That is, write what you see now, even if you don't understand what it means, for in the end its meaning will be revealed. Tomlinson and his church took this quite literally. They believed that they were living in that appointed time, "at the end," and that the visions of scripture (which its writers faithfully wrote down without fully understanding) were now being made plain. They believed that it was no accident, for example, that the Wright brothers first took flight in North Carolina in 1903, the same year in which Tomlinson became the leader of the Camp Creek congregation, and the same year he received a divine revelation on a nearby mountaintop of the restored New Testament church. For the airplane was the visible fulfillment of the prophet's vision of the winged chariot in the first chapter of Ezekiel. Soon the Church of God had amassed one hundred and ten planes, the "White Angel Fleet," which they used to drop tracts all over the world. Ezekiel didn't know what he was seeing in his vision, but Tomlinson and his followers believed that they did. They saw themselves as living in the final days before the return of Jesus, a time in which all the scriptures would be fulfilled, made plain in visible, concrete form.

Axis Mundi

Today, the most visible, concrete (and I do mean *concrete*) sign of Tomlinson's legacy with the Church of God of Prophecy is Fields of the Wood. Located on Highway 294 in western North Carolina, a few hundred yards north of Camp Creek and about eighteen miles east of the town of Murphy (in the news recently as the hiding place of Eric Robert Rudolph, who eluded the FBI for six years before his arrest in 2002 for bombing Atlanta's Centennial Olympic Park, an Atlanta women's clinic, and a gay nightclub), this two-hundred-and-sixteen-acre complex is both a visible sign of the church's presence in the world and a memorial to Tomlinson's inaugural vision.

Fields of the Wood was established as world headquarters of the Church of God of Prophecy in 1941, but the location's significance is rooted in the very beginnings of the movement. For it was there, in 1903, atop a mountain on the west side of the property, that Tomlinson had his original revelation of the restored New Testament church. Nearly forty years later, in his twilight years, Tomlinson led his church to establish Fields of the Wood to commemorate and sanctify that original revelation and to provide a cosmic center for the church itself. Fields of the Wood, then, is the Church of God of Prophecy's Mount Sinai and Jerusalem all rolled into one.

Even the name of the place, "Fields of the Wood," refers to the visible fulfillment of a biblical passage. Psalm 132 recalls how the Israelites recovered the Ark of the Lord and established it in Jerusalem after finding it in a place that the King James Version translates as "the fields of the wood" (most modern translations identify the place as the "fields of Jaar"). Most would read that to mean that the Israelites found the lost Ark in a field amid woods, a clearing. For Tomlinson and his followers, however, it was understood—or rather revealed—to be a reference to a specific place that would only be realized millennia later in the woods of North Carolina. "Fields of the Wood" became the proper name of the place where Tomlinson found the lost Apostolic church, prefigured by Israel's lost-and-found Ark of the Lord.

Like the New Jerusalem described in the New Testament book of Revelation (chapter 21), Fields of the Wood has twelve gates, three each in the north, south, east, and west, thereby presenting itself quite literally as the visible sign of the restored church, the New Jerusalem, of the final days. Seen from the air, these four sets of gates are also four ends of a cross that points roughly northward. Visitors enter through the large archway of the southern gate. The northern and southern gates are connected by a wide paved road and parking area that runs along a valley between two hills, forming the long vertical line of the cross.

In this north–south valley area are eighty-six flags, representing all the nations in which the Church of God of Prophecy has congregations, along with several installations, including: an aqua baptismal pool, which, if it weren't for the wrought-iron gate and wide white stairway on one end, would look very much like a backyard swimming pool; a Golgotha Crucifixion scene, made of concrete and piled stones with three neatly planed whitewashed crosses on top; and an empty tomb, complete with a perfectly round roll-away "stone," made of wood and covered with lumpy plaster for that much-sought-after rugged look. Inside the tomb I experienced one of the more disturbing moments of my travels. Behind a wrought-iron gate are two stone beds set parallel to one another on opposite walls. One is empty, but the other isn't. Lying there is a humanoid form on a wooden stretcher, covered top to bottom with a badly stained sheet. I presume this figure was placed there to be realistic. It is, after all, supposed to represent a burial place. What would be more surprising would be the empty bed, not the full one. Right? Be that as it may, children having fun rolling the stone away wouldn't find this nearly so amusing. I sternly advised mine not to go in.

Size Matters

The two east–west arms of the cross are formed by grassy areas that run up the hillsides of the valley, each touting at least one "world's largest" religious object made from concrete. Indeed, although I'm not sure whether there's much biblical theology to back it up, it's clear that size matters at Fields of the Wood.

Running up the western hill is a pathway lined on both sides with

Fields of the Wood, near Murphy, N.C.

Postcard of Aerial View, Fields of the Wood

large concrete slabs. Along the right side of the path are the Tables
of Bible Doctrines, which describe the central tenets of the Church
of God, such as eternal life for the righteous, eternal damnation for
the wicked, and prohibitions against personal adornment, swearing,
strong drink, and membership in lodges. Along the left side are the
Five Auxiliary Tables, which recount the major eras of ecclesiastical
history according to Church of God doctrine, beginning with the
New Testament church and its apostasy and culminating with the
"latter days" outpouring of the Holy Spirit in the Holiness and Pentecostal movement led by Tomlinson and others. At the top of the
path is the Place of Prayer, the centerpiece of which is "the World's
Largest Altar," eighty feet wide, marking the spot where Tomlinson
had his original vision of the restored church.

The western hill is not particularly well traveled by visitors, the
majority of whom, these days, are not Church-of-Godders. For most
visitors, the real attraction, the pièce de résistance, is on the eastern
hill. As Tomlinson reflected back on his life in his twilight years, he
came to believe that his original mountaintop experience was
prefigured in the Old Testament by the giving of the Ten Commandments to Moses on Mount Sinai. Not known for his modesty, Tomlinson saw Moses as his precursor and Israel as the precursor of the
Church of God. So it seemed appropriate that an image of the original law revealed to Moses be built on the hillside opposite the one
he descended after his revelation.

Behold, the World's Largest Ten Commandments. Written with
concrete block letters across the neatly mown east hillside in King
James Version English, its ten laws are divided into two tablet-
shaped sets of five. The letters themselves are about five feet tall and
the Roman numerals are about ten feet tall. Purportedly visible from
outer space, it draws Christians and a few curious others miles down

state highways and country roads to experience it for themselves in all its awesome glory.

Between the two tablets is a stairway from the parking lot to the top, where there sits yet another record-setting textual body: the World's Largest New Testament. Thirty feet high and fifty feet wide, this concrete book is opened to the Great Commandment from Matthew 22, to "love the Lord your God with all thy heart, with all thy soul, and with all thy mind" and to "love thy neighbor as thy self." On this, Jesus declared, hang all the law and all the prophets.

Awefully Big

Fields of the Wood hosts over a hundred thousand visitors every year, nearly all of them evangelical Christians. The complex is operated by seventeen full-time staff people and has an annual maintenance budget of $150,000, which is paid for by membership dues in the Church of God of Prophecy's Heritage Ministries. In the early years, almost all visitors were members of the church. Arriving from all over the country for annual general assemblies and other meetings, they would run through the gates, arms waving, speaking in tongues, rapt in the Holy Ghost. These days, however, the vast majority of visitors have nothing to do with Tomlinson's church. Most are Baptists. They arrive in tour buses and cars, placidly, sticky from long hot drives, with little or no visible signs of the spirit.

I parked our motor home in the lot at the base of the Ten Commandments. It was early morning, and the sun was just beginning to peek over the World's Largest New Testament above the World's Largest Ten Commandments. Gospel music was being broadcast from tinny loudspeakers like the ones used at county fairs. By ten in

World's Largest Ten Commandments, Fields of the Wood

the morning, a steady stream of cars and buses were pouring through the gates and filling the parking lots. Some visitors headed straight for the air-conditioned gift shop and café. Others gathered in a circle of folding chairs for a Bible study under a shade tent near the baptismal font. But most didn't leave the parking lot. They stood there, mouths hanging open in rapt awe, staring at the main attraction, the World's Largest Ten Commandments. What did they see?

"They can't be reading it," Sophie commented. "It's too big to read."

She was absolutely right. From the vantage point of the parking lot, this giant text is, let's say, *largely illegible*. You can recognize letters and Roman numerals, but it's nearly impossible to read whole commandments, let alone the whole Ten Commandments. You're too close. In order to make it legible, you need to gain some distance by climbing the stairs on the opposite hillside. Few that I saw in this predominantly older church crowd were even considering that. Besides, most were plenty familiar with the words, which are not semantically altered by size.

Indeed, whatever Tomlinson's original intention in creating it, the effect of this attraction has little to do with its theological *content*, the meaning of its actual text. It's not about saying the Ten Commandments in a big, loud way. It's about overwhelming viewers with illegible bigness. The intent here seems to be to elicit a religious experience of awe in the face of a sacred law that is overwhelmingly, *ineffably huge* in a most literal way.

As I mentioned earlier, Clover grew up in a small charismatic church, and continues to have a warm spot in her heart for that tradition. What endears her to that movement is its orientation toward the local congregation, the church family, and its base among working-class people of modest means and little formal education who live out their faith with integrity and sincerity. On the one hand, she says, people in this tradition have a kind of assurance of faith, which comes from the gifts of the spirit (tongues, for example). This is seen as a mark of the spirit's presence. On the other hand, there is a real humility among them, because salvation is never secure; it's a process of self-sanctification. Here at Fields of the Wood, with all its gigantic monuments and scriptural proof texts, she felt that that tension had been lost. The feeling this place conveys is one of spiritual superiority and spiritual security that you don't see on the ground in the real spiritual lives of people within this movement, who work out their salvation in fear and trembling, as the Apostle Paul put it. Here, it seems, charismatic enthusiasm about the presence of the spirit has been amplified into a kind of whitewashed hugeness that seems alien from the grassroots authenticity that marks local congregations within the movement.

Idolizing the Word

The proprietor of Fields of the Wood when we visited was Dr. Wade Phillips, who was also serving as a leading church historian of the Church of God of Prophecy and doing some teaching at the Church of God Theological Seminary in the nearby town of Cleveland, Tennessee. I met him in the café, where he was just finishing up a couple burger baskets for customers. "I'll be right with you, Tim," he said cheerfully with a warm southern accent. "Our cook is running late and I need to cover for him." The air-conditioned indoor dining area was full, so I waited at a picnic table outside. Eventually Dr. Phillips took off his cooking apron and joined me for a conversation about the story of Fields of the Wood, most of which I've already shared.

Although he can grill a burger or mop a floor when he needs to, Dr. Phillips is first and foremost a scholar, and his primary interest is in the history of the Church of God of Prophecy. He describes his own conversion to Christianity, nearly forty years ago, as beginning with a very deeply felt "desire to know," and his entire ministry has been one of historical research, which he has carried out with great passion. Indeed, one of the things that attracted him to the position of church historian at Fields of the Wood was that it allowed him to conduct primary research on the early history of Tomlinson and the holiness movement in local church archives and through personal interviews with Church of God old-timers.

As a leader in a movement whose history he studies, Dr. Phillips's scholarly research and his personal faith life are inseparable. Indeed, he sees himself as a reformer. He expressed particular concern that Fields of the Wood has become something of a sacred center, a "Salt Lake City or Mecca," as he put it, for the Church of God of Prophecy. He's absolutely right: as I suggested earlier, it is both Mount Sinai and Jerusalem. Seeing such a sanctification of this place as "cultish," he was working to make it more of a center of historical education for the church. Although put in conservative Christian terms that Clover would not use, he was expressing a concern about this place that was very similar to hers—namely, that the living spirituality of the charismatic movement was here being in some way monumentalized into a concrete institutional form of spiritual dominance. Put another way, we might say that Dr. Phillips worries that the movement's early twentieth-century revival and reawakening that began with the movement of the Spirit, which goes where it will, now finds itself sacramentally set in concrete. The visible sign of the church here at Fields of the Wood is at risk of becoming a graven image in itself.

Dr. Phillips's concern reflects a deep-seated conviction, shared by many conservative Protestants, that Christianity, unlike other religions, is essentially immaterial, even antimaterial. In fact, many Protestants insist that Christianity is not a "religion" at all. To get back to the New Testament church is to get out from under all the "cultish" layers of tradition—those sensual smells and bells and sacred grounds that have smothered right doctrine with religious aesthetics. For Phillips and many other Protestants, human fascination with the materiality of religion seduces Christians away from the true foundations of faith, which are essentially dogmatic and grounded in the Word, not the *image*. Too much focus on the things and images of Christian tradition leads to the sin of idolatry.

Since our visit, Dr. Phillips has left his position at Fields of the Wood and broken from the Church of God of Prophecy. Convinced that that church is neglecting some of its oldest and most fundamental principles, he has started a new church in nearby Cleveland, Tennessee. It would be understandable if part of Dr. Phillips's reason for leaving was also frustration in the battle against "cultish" idolatry at Fields of the Wood. He certainly had his work cut out for him there.

Whether or not we identify with the fundamentalist aversion

to the material aesthetics of Christianity (I don't), it's doubtful that Fields of the Wood will ever free itself entirely from its sanctification of material objects. Indeed, if anything, what Fields of the Wood has done is make the Word into a material idol. If you climb the hill opposite the World's Largest Ten Commandments, so that you can read them, you'll note that the Second Commandment is the prohibition against idolatry: "Thou shalt not make unto thee any graven image." In its reverent display of this and the other nine commandments, it seems to me that Fields of the Wood idolizes the Word itself. It has turned the Ten Commandments, with their prohibition against graven images, into a graven image—"the World's Largest," in fact.

Not that it's a graven image of God her- or himself. Yet the Ten Commandments themselves, which for many Christians symbolize the Word of God, holy scripture, are here concretized as a sacred object, eliciting a worshipful response of reverence, awe, even praise. What compels and overwhelms visitors about the World's Largest Ten Commandments is not what they say but how big they are. This ginormous text does not assert its theological content so much as it overwhelms the senses. It does not elicit a theological or doctrinal experience, a revelation of the authoritative truth of scripture or divine law. Rather it elicits an aesthetic religious experience of the Word of God as image, and I dare say idol.

In even the most iconoclastic religious traditions, sacred objects and images have ways of getting around all the prohibitions against them. One way is by making the written word itself *into* a sacred image, thereby undermining the priority of word over image. In Islamic and Jewish calligraphy, for example, we find images of texts that are so ornately beautiful that they are nearly unreadable. The aesthetics of the word as image has overtaken its literary content. Bordering on illegibility, the word has essentially become image.

Granted, the Word made image at Fields of the Wood is not nearly so beautiful as these Islamic and Jewish calligraphic texts. Yet, as a remarkable instance of the return of the religiously suppressed, these giant hillside tablets do deserve a prize for irony, making a graven image of the prohibition against graven images. Not that irony is much prized among those biblicists most susceptible to this particular form of it, whether we find them gazing in awe at the massive Roman numerals on the hillside of Fields of the Wood or kneeling in a prayer circle around the Alabama state Judicial Building wherein Chief Justice Roy Moore was fighting to keep his 5300-pound monument of the two tablets prominently and reverently displayed.

Near the lower right-hand corner of the second tablet, next to the Tenth Commandment, there are three life-size concrete sheep. One is lying down, its head turned toward the parking lot, and the other two are grazing in the dry, pale green grass. Pastoral images of peace and contentment, they are sinking ever so gradually into the ground. Their legs are no longer visible, and the faces of the two that are grazing are burrowed underground as though they're grubbing for worms. More than a half-century of gravity must be having the same effect on the Ten Commandments themselves. Eventually, without some major digging and foundation work, they will bury themselves on that hillside. Perhaps, in the end, nature will be Dr. Phillips's greatest ally in deterring idolatry at Fields of the Wood.

As we climbed the stairs between the two tablets a little dog came trotting our way along the grass above number V, "Honor thy father and mother." She was clearly a new mother and had left her nursing puppies in the woods somewhere in search of food. Her ribs and hips poked out of her mangy coat. She looked to be starving. Sophie and Seth ran to meet her and soon had made fast friends. Realizing how hungry she was, and that she had puppies somewhere, they took her on as their mission for the day, buying her food and playing

Sinking Sheep, Fields of the Wood

with her on the grassy slopes of the Ten Commandments. Whenever she would trot over near the gift shop and café, the kids close behind, she was shooed away by clapping and yelling visitors. Witnessing this, Sophie and Seth were filled with righteous indignation. To this day, ask them about Fields of the Wood and they won't tell you about the baptismal pool, or the rolling stone in front of the tomb, or even the huge Ten Commandments. They'll tell you about the stray mother dog and how poorly she was treated. "These people say they're Christians, and they treated that dog like that," Seth said, his voice shaking with anger. For our kids, as the Commandments were amplified, another more important biblical lesson had been ignored: "Truly I say to you, just as you did not do it to one of the least of these, you did not do it to me" (Matthew 25:45).

Chapter Six

ΠΕ∫ΤΙΠ6 HΛBΙΤ∫

Cross Garden
Prattville, Alabama

These days most Americans think of gardens as private backyard spaces of retreat or leisure, patches of plants, thoughtfully placed stones, wrought iron, trellises, and other complementary décor. Yet traditionally gardens in the West had far more symbolic import. They were conceived as microcosms of creation, constructs of the theological imagination, spaces of moral reflection and spiritual inspiration—"gardens of revelation," to borrow John Beardsley's apt phrase from his book of the same title. Such spaces provided those who created and inhabited them with what he calls a "language of spiritual or philosophical rumination."

A visual cacophony of scrap wood and old appliances spread out on either side of County Road 86 near Prattville, Alabama, Cross Garden (a.k.a. Rice's Crossgarden and House of Crosses) is anything but a garden in the contemporary American sense. Huge crosses made of skinned logs tower above the road from a bluff. Below these, nearer the road, are many more crosses, tilting this way and that along with plywood boards and metal boxes bearing words of divine judgment, death and hellfire: READ THE BIBLE, HPOCRITES, YOU WILL DIE, HELL HELL HELL HOT HOT, RICH MAN IN HELL REPENT.

Across the road from this display is a dirt pullout in which a small chapel-like shack sits. Above its door a sign reads, CHURCH OF GOD

JESUS AND THE HOLY GHOST, and all over its walls are more reminders that hell is indeed hot and that you will indeed die. On the door, written in foot-high letters, is the question, WHAT WILL YOU DO WITH JESUS?

Next to the church, a few broken-down top-loading laundry machines stand in a line, each with a wooden cross rising from its open lid. Such an unexpected combination of religious symbol and household appliance simultaneously demands and defies interpretation. Washed in the blood, maybe?

In front of the rambler-style home, just past the air-conditioner housings lined up along the driveway, is another concentration of crosses, signs, and ramshackle buildings surrounded by a barbed wire fence. Here the signage is slightly less hellish and more salvation-oriented: JESUS IS THE REASON FOR THE SEASON, JESUS SAVES, JESUS WILL HELP YOU.

Not your typical garden scene, in any case. Indeed, I doubt that the creator and proprietor of Cross Garden, William C. Rice, has ever set foot in a nursery or Home Depot. Yet this is a garden, albeit a heterodox one, in the more traditional sense described by Beardsley. It is a garden of revelation, a material expression of Mr. Rice's own very unique religious imagination.

Cross Garden is an otherworldly environment, an uncanny space which has the power to envelop visitors. Although the individual pieces of Cross Garden struck me as laughably makeshift and shoddy, the overall effect of this eleven-acre collage was overwhelming. I had seen pictures of the place in newspaper articles and on offbeat travel Web sites, so I thought I knew what to expect. I was wrong. You don't behold Cross Garden like an object in a picture frame. You don't take it in. It takes you in. It's total. Although not an enclosed space, there is, nonetheless, an architecture to it, a fantastic architecture, that gives one the feeling of enclosure.

Despairing Fridge, Cross Garden

Within this fantastic architecture, I was able to identify certain structural and spatial elements by which Cross Garden creates this enveloping, otherworldly experience. First, and perhaps most obviously, scale is important. When standing near the house, crosses and other objects are scattered in every direction as far as the eye can see. They fill every horizon, giving the eye no escape from this world. There are no outside points of reference. There is no objective viewpoint, no way to gain perspective distance. Like Dorothy in the enchanted forest, one feels subjected to its world of crosses, which seem to be alive, gazing down from bluffs and up from ditches.

Second, the signage has the effect of barraging the visitor with urgent messages, creating a felt need to respond, to answer, without any idea *how* to do so, other than to chuckle nervously. The place is literally saturated with intimidating written messages, most of them urgent warnings of impending hellfire, most often put in forms of personal address (YOU WILL DIE. WHAT WILL YOU DO?). Writing is all over the place. There are almost no blank spaces, and therefore there is little room for one's own thoughts or words. It fills one's consciousness.

Third, although in many ways radically unnatural, Cross Garden is also integrated into its natural environment. On the one hand, the text-ridden crosses and scraps and junk impose themselves on the land and all that grows there naturally. Just about anything that can hold a nail is covered with signage. Running up the trunk of a small tree near the house, for example, are sixteen signs, each with the word CROSS hastily painted on it in white, as though the tree has been relabeled, as though nature has been overwritten. On the other hand, many of the objects in Cross Garden appear to be assimilating to their natural environment. The crosses tilt this way and that like trees. Weathered from years of exposure, their colors blend with the grays of dead wood and the red-browns of the soil. It is both contrastive and complementary, simultaneously a part of the natural landscape and a contradiction of it.

Yet I don't think we can go so far as to call these structural and spatial elements "strategies," which would imply some degree of intentionality. The power of this space to envelop visitors is difficult to attribute to the conscious aims of its creator, Bill Rice. For it appears to have come together, or rather accrued, over a long period of time, almost by accident. I'm reminded of the brainstorming exercises I do on chalkboards with my college students, free-associating a web of words and phrases that spreads out in all directions. Cross Garden looks like a quarter-century-long brainstorming exercise. Except instead of words on a chalkboard we see words on crosses and boards and washing machines and air conditioner housings, spread out across eleven acres of yellow grass and brown-red Alabama soil.

Standing in the middle of Cross Garden, I felt as though I were standing in another's spiritual imaginary. It is an architecture of mind, a mind that is radically unfamiliar, perhaps ultimately uninterpretable. I felt as though I were in someone else's head without any sense of orientation, completely at a loss. An emotional space that I experienced as quite other than my own. It is a netherworld, at once compelling and unnerving.

A religious stream of consciousness seems to be running through this garden, welling up from some undetermined, unconscious source of creativity. It was above all the desire to follow that stream that kept me from running back to the motor home and hitting the road.

Family Room

Bill's wife, Marzell, saw me wandering among the crosses and rusty appliances in her front yard and came out to greet me. She welcomed me into the house and asked me to sign the guest book. Although I saw no other visitors during my day at Cross Garden, the guestbook had hundreds of pages of rows of names and addresses accompanied by comments like "Hell is hot!" and "Wow!"

Marzell found me a chair in the small, dimly lit family room and went to the bedroom to get Bill. I tried in vain to take in my surroundings. I dare say there were as many crosses in that room as there were outside. The walls were covered with them. They hung from the low ceiling. They lay on end tables and hearths and countertops. Many were actually crucifixes, that is, occupied crosses, on which crucified Jesuses were nailed in full pre-Resurrection abjection, crowned with thorns, faces contorted in agony, bodies bent in pain.

On the wall opposite me was an old high-school yearbook picture of one of the Rice boys, his smiling face peeking through a thicket of crosses that appeared to be growing over him like creeping kudzu. Judging from the width of the boy's lapel and the size of his bowtie, I'd date the picture circa Class of 1976.

I wasn't sure what to expect from this meeting with Bill. When I called the day before my visit to remind him that I was coming, an older man answered.

"Is this Mr. Rice?"

"No, no, this is Mr. Browning," he replied in a thick southern Alabama drawl. "Mr. Rice isn't home. He's gone to the store with his wife. Try back later if you want."

I called back an hour later and got the same man. But this time he admitted that he was in fact Mr. Rice, not Mr. Browning. "I lied earlier," he confessed, his voice cracking. "When you called back then I just couldn't talk. Sometimes I get so depressed, so tired from my diabetes [pronounced *dah-bee-teez*]. Do you forgive me, brother? I'd get on my knees right now, talking to you on the phone, if I could."

I assured him that I wasn't offended, that I understood how it can be sometimes. He thanked me profusely and declared that we were now good friends.

If I hadn't been apprehensive about the next day's visit before this phone exchange, I was afterward. At the same time, I was already beginning to see the author of Cross Garden as a rather fragile, vulnerable human being, fraught with inner struggles.

Eventually Bill shuffled into the room and gently sat down in the motorized recliner next to me. He was tall but bent and weakened by age, back trouble, and complications related to his diabetes. He had a Colonel Sanders beard and warm blue eyes. Marzell watched over him closely, serving as both nurse and religious attendant.

"Don't forget your cross and ribbons. He never talks to guests without wearing his ribbons and cross," she explained as she adorned him with his priestly vestments: four nylon ribbon necklaces on which little crosses had been drawn in black marker, a foot-long crucifix covered head to toe with tiny red drops, and a wide-brimmed black felt hat likewise decorated with crosses and ribbons.

Now properly vested, Bill leaned back and took a minute or two to catch his breath while Marzell gave me a packet of evangelical tracts and local newspaper articles about Cross Garden. "Bet you never seen this many crosses in your life!" Marzell began with a warm and sympathetic smile.

"So you're a teacher?" Bill interrupted. "You teach art? We get lots of art teachers and art students coming out here. People call this art. But I don't." I was aware that Cross Garden had received attention from art students and critics interested in outsider art. But I was interested in him and his place more in terms of outsider religion. I explained that I was a religion professor and that I'd like to know the story behind Cross Garden. His blue eyes warmed with new energy and interest as he gave his personal testimony, which is essentially the story of his lifework, Cross Garden.

One Cross at a Time

Born in Woodstock, Alabama, in 1930, Bill didn't "get saved and filled with the Holy Ghost" until 1960, while working as a house painter in Fort Rucker. As he tells the story, it was two in the morning and he was sitting in the kitchen of their trailer, chewing tobacco and suffering mightily from stomach ulcers. "I really was living it up for the devil wasn't I?" The next thing he knew, Jesus came into his heart, at which point "I came out of that chair, I spit tobacco all over the refrigerator, it went all over the floor, and he healed my ulcerated stomach." That was his "spiritual birthday," as he called it, and from that day forward he devoted his life to Christian evangelism, preaching to anyone who'd listen from a little red Datsun pickup that he had painted bumper to bumper with crosses and Bible verses. The Datsun still sits in the back yard. Turns out it was a foretaste of things to come.

Cross Garden didn't begin with his own spiritual birthday, however, but in 1977, with the spiritual birthdays of his parents, both of whom converted on their deathbeds. Shortly after his mother and father died (and were born again), Bill felt called by God to put up his first cross.

"God started me out small," he said as he pointed to the space above the back door near the kitchen, where three business-card-size tracts were tacked to the wall in the shape of a cross. On one card was a Bible verse, John 3:16, along with the statement, "This

Rice's Front Yard, Cross Garden

black cloth is in remembrance of God's son." On the other two are the names and dates of his parents, laid out like a tombstone, followed by prayers thanking God for saving them. So each of these three cards that come together to form the first cross of Cross Garden is both an acknowledgment of death—a little tombstone-like memorial—and a proclamation of victory over death.

The death of a parent can bring the reality of one's own inevitable death home in a most profound way. For Bill, I think, the deaths of both his parents within a single year did just that. At the same time, as an evangelical born-againer, he was supposed to rejoice that they were saved in the nick of time. The result for him, I think, was an experience of inner tension between grief and joy that goes to the very core of Christian faith and that is symbolized most profoundly by the Cross. On the one hand, the Cross is an instrument of torturous death. On the other hand, it symbolizes victory over death through Jesus's Crucifixion and Resurrection. Like the lamb's blood smeared on the doors of the Hebrew slaves' homes in Egypt, it protects the household from the angel of death who would pass over. For Bill, then, that first cross, made of three tombstone-like memorials to Jesus, Mama, and Daddy, signifies not only death knocking at his door, death come home, but also death's Passover. That first cross was an expression both of the inevitability of death, of life as being-toward-death, and of faith in that which might overcome death. At the founding of Cross Garden, then, is a profound but not quite consciously acknowledged experience of the tension between being-toward-death and being-toward-life, between terror of the abyss and hope for salvation.

Soon after putting the first cross on the wall, Bill felt the call again. This time God told him to plant three wooden crosses, Calvary style, in his front yard. "It was the hardest thing I ever done," Bill said. "It hurt in my chest to do it." He dreaded what neighbors and passersby would think. But as the calls to plant more and more crosses came, his anxieties about what neighbors might think faded. Twenty-seven years later we see what it's come to: thousands of crosses, scrap boards, and discarded appliances bearing messages warning that the end of the world is near, that sex is hell, that hell is hot and offers no refreshments, and that Jesus saves.

Where does Bill get his ideas for Cross Garden? He told me that God almost always gives him directions in night visions. While sleeping, he'll see a whole new installation in minute detail, as though already completed: air conditioner housings, for example, painted with specific messages about how there's no ice water in hell, running up his driveway. As soon as the dream vision ends, he awakes with a start, wakes up Marzell, and tells her exactly what he's seen. "I just can't wait till morning. I can't wait to get it done."

These days, however, turning dreams into realities is increasingly difficult. Bill and Marzell are now in their seventies, and Bill's diabetes has become severely debilitating. So they depend heavily on help from their adult children, especially Jerry who lives in a trailer in their backyard. "The kids, they all back him up," Marzell explained. "They back him all the way. They're all making crosses too, just like he tells them to."

"That's the part I was getting up to," Bill interrupted. "That's another gift God give me. God showed me that all my immediate family, they get to get saved. Just like Noah's family, who got to get saved with Noah in the Ark. So I don't have to worry about that."

With this revelation, I began to see Cross Garden as something of a modern-day Ark, with Bill as its Noah. Granted, this eleven-acre collage of crosses and broken appliances bearing proclamations of immanent divine judgment won't float when the floodwaters begin to rise. But Bill is nonetheless building it in the hope of surviving perdition with his family intact. Like Noah, who was called to build the Ark in preparation for divine judgment on the world's unrighteous masses, Bill feels that God is calling him to build Cross Garden as a warning of immanent divine judgment on a world gone bad. But inside, he and his family are safe and secure, protected from the storm.

Discourse on the Origin of Ideas

"Now ask me some more questions," he declared, apparently revved up after telling his story. "You ask me questions, and I'll give you Bible answers."

"Tell me more about Noah. Do you see yourself as a modern-day Noah?"

"Well, Noah is the best one to compare with this here. God give me signs, like he give Noah. Like about four weeks ago he give me one. God said, 'the world coming to a end.' So now, now, he's got that out there. He's got that coming to me." Recall the large message written in capital letters across several crosses on the bluff outside: GOD SAID THE WORLD COMING TOO A END. From God's sign to Bill to Bill's sign in Cross Garden. Now God's got that out there.

Which raises an interesting question, one that continues to captivate theologians, psychologists, cognitive scientists, and neuroscientists alike: Where do new ideas come from?

Our word "idea" derives from the Greek verb *idein*, "to see." A new idea is a new and unexpected way of seeing something, a new mental picture. When I have a new idea, I feel as though it hits me from out of the blue. Upon further reflection, I can usually identify many of its more or less loosely associated components—images and words and feelings that have been shuffling around in my mind. It's like a chemical accident in which surprising new properties emerge from combining elements in new ways. But when these components come together, converge, gel in the form of a new idea, I'm invariably taken by surprise. It feels like an in-breaking of something other, something extra-mental. A revelation.

These days most of us, postreligious post-Freudians that we are, chalk such ideational miracles up to the behind-the-scenes workings of the unconscious or subconscious mind, that inaccessible and ultimately mysterious realm within. In cognitive-psychological terms, an idea is an *intra-mental* event, an expression of a brain state, brought about by largely unknown processes of patterning, synthesizing, blending, and so on. Note that although this way of explaining an idea attributes its emergence to intra-mental processes, the process that leads to the birth of a new idea, a new way of seeing, remains a mystery. Still strangers to ourselves, most of us continue to posit the source of new ideas, the wellspring of creativity, as a mysterious otherness within.

But for Bill, ideas are extra-mental. They come from outside, from the mind of God. He receives a new idea, blindsiding his mind's eye from out of nowhere, as a gift from God, a divine revelation.

Bill certainly isn't the first to think of ideas this way. In fact, the theory that ideas come from some transcendent realm has a long and distinguished history, going back at least as far as Plato, who understood human ideas to be apprehensions of universal Ideas, or Forms, which exist outside the human mind in a celestial realm of archetypes. Drawing on Plato, early Christian theologians understood such universal Ideas to exist in the mind of God, as the archetypal forms or patterns used by the divine Author of the universe, according to which all the species of creation were made. For them, ideas were believed to be creative thoughts of God. To apprehend them is to apprehend the mind of God in the form of divine revelation.

Granted, these theologians were talking about big ideas—the "universal ideas" that provide the blueprint for creation, not ideas for decorating with old washing machines. But Bill Rice's implicit theory of ideas as divine revelations rather than as products of intramental processes certainly resonates with this long tradition of understanding ideas theologically, as concepts residing in the creative mind of God and apprehended, "seen," by individual human minds in moments of illumination.

Ark Nest

Despite his faint voice, shortness of breath, and Alabama drawl, I found Bill's manner of speaking most compelling. It's a kind of informal preaching that meanders from one biblical image to another. His mind seemed to me to be immersed in a biblical pool of imagination, his words flowing from his mouth in a homiletical stream of consciousness as he stared dreamily into space. Billy Graham meets James Joyce.

"All them spirits. I talk to all them spirits all the time. You know, if you're talking to one of them spirits you're talking to all of them. It's all just one big family up there. They don't have no cars up there, nobody getting drunk and killing people, they don't have no mercantile, don't know none of that up there. That's a happy place." While saying this, Bill stared into my eyes, smiling dreamily, apparently relishing this otherworldly vision of sober yet happy spirits without the worries of cars, drunk drivers, and consumerism.

"Don't forget about Noah, Bill," Marzell interrupted from a nearby sofa, recalling him to my question. "Tell him all about Noah now."

"Well, God give me a talent," he began. "You know the Bible story of the talents?" I nodded. He was referring to the parable in the Gospel of Matthew about the three servants who were given talents by their master to invest while he was away on a long journey. One was given five, another two, and another one, each according to his ability. When the servants reported back about what they did with their talents, the master condemned the servant who buried his one talent for safekeeping and greatly praised the other two for doubling theirs through risky investments. It's a parable that calls for risk-taking faith, double or nothing. Bill sees himself as having been given relatively little and taking a great and risky leap of faith with it.

Now a talent in first-century Palestine was worth about one hundred pounds of silver, more than fifteen years of wages for a laborer. No doubt the homonym with our word for ability has contributed to the popularity of this parable among English-speaking Christians. As a child I remember hearing this parable in Sunday school often. Always I pictured a shining token that somehow actually represented a special gift of ability. I'm sure other kids did too. And I don't remember Sunday school teachers ever trying to correct this accidental convergence of currency and ability. Neither was I about to interrupt Bill's parabolic testimony with any such point.

"God give me one talent—painting," Bill said. Not five or three, but just one, according to his modest ability. Then he turned and fixed his gaze sharply on me. "*Just like he give Noah a talent.* Noah used his to build that Ark. And I'm building this here."

"Now this here place," he continued, "it's not finished. Maybe it never will be. You see it's not up to me when to stop. And that's like Noah too. Because God told him to build that Ark. And God decided when it was done. Who shut up the Ark when it was time? Not Noah. God did it. God shut the door on that Ark when he had it the way he wanted it." Bill was referring to the point in the biblical narrative, just before the floodgates of heaven were opened, when God shut the Ark's one little opening. For Bill, then, it was up to God to say when Cross Garden was finished. Bill conceived of himself and

his family as implementers of divine creativity. In Bill's mind, this
is God's work in progress. Bill's God likes to build unusual things
for humanity to contemplate—arks, eleven-acre collages—before
he lays waste to the world.

At that point, perhaps remembering the dove that returned to
Noah with the olive branch when the flooding had begun to subside,
Bill made an abrupt shift that took me by surprise. "Like a bird's
nest," he said. "The bird gets a twig, and then a twig . . . a twig . . . and
another. Little by little, twig by twig. They don't do it all in a single
day. They don't make that nest like that." And then, eyes wide, smiling, finger pointing at me, he said, "And you know what? He never
give me that one before. He just give me that one right here! That
illustration from nature, about a bird building a nest." It took me a
second to realize what he meant: God had just revealed to him, for
the first time, this illustration of Cross Garden as a work-in-progress
akin to a bird's nest. "That's the way it happens," he continued, com-
menting on the divine revelation I had apparently just witnessed.
"He talks to me, like we talking now. He gives me all kinds . . . different things. And I just got that one! Bird's nest. I never thought
about it that way before. How 'bout that? That's a good one. It
works, don't it?" I had just witnessed the coming of an idea.

Cross Garden is an Ark, and Bill is its Noah. But this Ark is also
a nest, built slowly and carefully, piece by piece, from scraps of wood
and other discards, a safe haven protected from the storm gathering
all around.

Outsider

Considered as a work of outsider art and outsider religion, Bill Rice's
Cross Garden raises a question central in the study of religion: What
is the relationship between creative vision and social marginality?

Does social marginalization lead to alternative ways of seeing, or do alternative ways of seeing lead to social marginalization? Does seeing otherwise make you socially other, or does being socially other make you see otherwise?

This question is as pertinent to Bill Rice as it is to those biblical prophets that operated on the margins of society, such as Ezekiel and John of Patmos (to whom the New Testament book of Revelation is attributed). To what extent might their highly disturbing, often extremely violent visions be the result of their marginal social status? Indeed, John's marginal status is clear from his text: he writes while in exile on the island of Patmos and identifies with a Christian community experiencing aggressive Roman persecution. On the other hand, perhaps the disturbingly "other" visions of these prophets are the cause of their marginal status. In fact, some have hypothesized that both of these prophetic figures, John of Patmos and Ezekiel, suffered from something similar to modern-day paranoid schizophrenia.

Does Bill see what he sees and do what he does because he lives and moves and has his being so far outside the dominant norms of religion and culture—including its norms of psychological health, according to which he would certainly be diagnosed as something other than a religious visionary? Does his stream of consciousness curl its way into such unusual and fascinating eddies of thought precisely because it flows so far from the mainstream? Or is it the other way around? Is it his alternative way of seeing and being that has, over the years, left him free-floating far outside the current? Such questions, of course, must always outlive the answers we give them. But for Bill, I imagine, the answer is certain: whatever marginalization he experiences is on account of his vision, which was given by God. And this, of course, can only lead to more marginalization, and the desire to build the walls of the nest/Ark thicker.

As I stood to accept a glass of lemonade from Marzell, Bill noticed that I was carrying a video camera. Could I shoot a video of him, he wondered. "I'd like to give a message to your students." I readily agreed. We set up the video and he started to talk, rambling at first, apparently looking for a current of thought to catch. "I got a man and a wife and their two kids visiting me and talking the other day," he began, though he had yet to meet Clover and the kids. "And we's having a time, we was talking together about this place. And it's amazing for people to see how it's put together. Like we was talking a while ago about like a bird . . . that's a good . . . that's the first time I had that. I was telling a while ago. When I was talking to you. That's the reason why, that's the reason why it don't come to no end, see. God just keeps giving you something. That's the way he does to me. And I, . . . he hasn't given me that before. Just like a bird with a nest."

When he got to this point in the illustration, however, he took it in a different direction, one that gave expression, I think, to his self-understanding as being not-of-this-world, his fragility in the face of death, and his hope for new life. This time, he compared God, not himself, to a bird building its nest. God was the mother bird and Cross Garden was her nest, in which she protected and fed Bill and his family like vulnerable baby birds. "He," that is, the mother bird, God, "made it just the way he want it. He put stuff out there for them to eat, and they don't starve to death. He takes care of us."

Lift High the Cross

Bill Rice isn't the only one who has felt called to plant crosses by the side of the road. In 1984, the late self-proclaimed Reverend Bernard Coffindaffer was given a vision to use the revenues from his coal-washing business in West Virginia to plant trios of wooden crosses—one gold flanked by two blue—along highways and interstates throughout the United States and beyond. By 1993, when he died, he and his crews had planted 1,864 clusters of crosses.

Whereas Reverend Coffindaffer went for high numbers, others apparently believe size matters most. There are numerous giant roadside crosses in the United States, including the 190-foot cross in Groom, Texas, and the 198-foot illuminated "Cross at the Crossroads," framed with steel and finished with vinyl siding, at the intersection of Interstates 57 and 70 in Effingham, Illinois.

Such cruciform erections, many and huge, along the rural highways and interstates of America tend to strike me primarily as expressions of Christian imperialism. This is God's land, they seem to declare. This is a Christian nation. Such crosses stake property, mark territory, and express dominance.

Not so Cross Garden. This project has less to do with staking claims and marking territory than it does with nesting. Granted, Cross Garden means to get the attention of passersby, to wake them up and get them saved before it's too late. Hell, after all, is hot hot hot. But it's also a deeply personal work. Bill is building a nest of crosses. He is nestled in crosses. It's his sanctuary, in both senses of the word: a sacred place and a shelter. Crosses, scrap board signs, and dumped appliances are the twigs, leaves, and bread-ties of this nest. Cross Garden is a nest of crosses, sheltering vulnerable lives within it, keeping them warm and dry as the hard rain falls.

Chapter Seven

ISN'T IT JUST PRECIOUS?

Precious Moments Inspiration Park
Carthage, Missouri

As I write I am drinking coffee from my favorite morning mug. On it is a light, wispy, pastel painting of a little girl with that trademark Precious Moments look, made famous by the porcelain bisque figurines that have been bestsellers at Hallmark stores and other gift shops for more than two decades. She's wearing a frilly calico dress with a light yellow pattern. Her head, mostly forehead, is several times larger than her torso, teetering on a neck narrower than her wrist. She has a tiny nose and mouth, and gigantic, wide-set, teardrop-shaped eyes. Her dress pocket has the word *Seeds* printed on it in a simple script as though written with a magic marker by the girl so she doesn't forget what she's carrying. She's walking in a field of flowers, dropping acorns and other seeds onto the ground as a few birds flit around at her feet, pecking gratefully. The caption underneath the scene, written in the same script as the word on her pocket, reads, "The Lord will provide." An interesting image of God, I suppose: a little girl sowing seeds to sustain the Earth and Earth's creatures, although I must admit I've never really thought about that until just now.

I don't know where I got this mug. It must have been a gift from my grandmother or one of my great aunts. It's been in our cupboard for almost twenty years. It was pretty high up on the Salvation Army giveaway list when I discovered it ten years or so ago and made it my own. I like this cup because it's so not me. It's so simple, so guileless, so unironic. It's something I'm far from being able to put my finger on, or point my finger at.

For a great many people, the porcelain bisque figurines and paintings of big-headed, big-eyed children and child angels that make up the Precious Moments family are deeply meaningful and highly treasured. What makes these images of innocent, open, and trusting interaction with the world so appealing, so touching, so, well, *precious* to so many? On first impression, one might suspect that they speak to one's nostalgia for a childlike way in the world that has been lost. They represent lost innocence, wonder, faith. Perhaps. But when you talk with the people who love them, they give a different answer. They say that the figures represent what's really in their hearts. They reveal the childlike vulnerability that they actually feel inside now in relation to the world outside.

Indeed, the "world outside" in which Precious Moments figurines are depicted is not always a precious world, not always a nice world. Often these figures are depicted interacting with catastrophe, cruelty, and human suffering that raise big questions about the meaning of life and the presence, or absence, of God in the world, questions that most people simply don't have words to ask, let alone answer. Often, moreover, the responses of these precious figures convey not naive trust but confusion and pain. There's a Precious Moments drawing in a book of biblical reflections that depicts a child kneeling down on the ground to touch the prick of what we (but not he) know to be a crown of thorns. A very popular porcelain figurine depicts a teary-eyed blond boy sitting at a small desk with a phone to his ear. At his feet is a sheet of paper that reads, "Dear Jon, I'm sorry to . . ." The name of this figurine, written on its base, is "Hello, Lord, it's me again." Another boy, wearing a firefighter's hat and yellow firefighter's coat, stands amid pieces of charred concrete rubble and a teddy bear with a bandage on its forehead. At the base are the words, "Remember the children. Oklahoma City 1995." In his arms is a little baby draped in a blanket, eyes closed. A tear rolls down the firefighter's left cheek and his mouth is drawn in a small red circle, expressing shock and confusion. Many will recall the famous photo that must have inspired this figure: a firefighter emerging from the rubble of the Oklahoma City bombing on April 19, 1995, carrying the body of one-year-old Baylee Almon in his arms. Here in this Precious Moments memorial, the man has become a child, carrying a child, revealing the trauma of the moment, a trauma brought on by the suffering face of an innocent and infinitely vulnerable human being in a world of indiscriminate and explosive violence.

People sometimes tell of getting hooked on Precious Moments figures when someone gave them one to mark a particular occasion or life experience—a "precious moment." It may have been a happy event, but often it wasn't. Many times it's the death of a spouse or child or close friend. In any case, the figure comes to memorialize and speak to the moment in a way the person otherwise can't. And it does so with disarming vulnerability and sincerity. No highfalutin interpretations of the meaning of it all, just an expression of simple, raw feeling.

Sam Butcher

By all accounts, Samuel J. Butcher, the man behind the Precious Moments phenomenon, is himself an unabashedly open, vulnerable, emotionally expressive soul.

Sam, as he is always called by Precious Moments enthusiasts, was born on New Year's Day 1939 in Jackson, Michigan, and moved with his family to Redding, California, at age ten. Marginalized within his family, which he describes as dysfunctional, Sam never identified with his father's work as a mechanic, preferring to paint pictures rather than cars with the automotive paint in the garage. Despite the lack of encouragement from his father, he managed to do well in school and win a scholarship to the California College of Arts and Crafts. He and his wife, Katie, had their first child in 1962, and he had to leave college before finishing his degree in order to support his new family.

In 1963, he had a conversion experience, and soon took a job in "chalk ministry" (a form of evangelism that involves speaking while illustrating the lesson in chalk art) for Child Evangelism Fellowship in Grand Rapids, Michigan. There he met William Biel, and in 1975 the two started a Christian greeting-card business called Jonathan and David (named after the friendship of the biblical David and King Saul's son Jonathan, who gave up his right to the throne for his friend). They first developed a Precious Moments series of cards, featuring Sam's paintings of the now well-known figures, for an international convention of the Christian Booksellers Association. The cards were explosively popular and soon were discovered by Eugene Freedman, president of Enesco Corporation in the giftware industry. Freedman recruited Japanese sculptor Yasuhei Fujioka to create the first porcelain bisque prototypes based on Sam's artwork. Sam and Bill immediately fell in love with them. By fall 1978 the first series of figures hit the market and was hugely popular. Precious Moments soon became a giftware phenomenon like none before it. As the figurine business grew, Sam turned his full attention to working with Enesco on creating and producing Precious Moments figures, while William Biel returned exclusively to the greeting-card business.

A quarter of a century later, Enesco's Precious Moments line continues to thrive. Now sixty-five years old, Sam lives in the Philippines, where apparently there is good clay, and is as closely involved with creation and production as ever.

Sam is often quoted as saying that Precious Moments (referring not only to the figures but to precious moments in life) are born of great happiness and great sorrow. His figures are intended to mark and memorialize peak moments of joy and pain in order to make them more precious.

Sam himself has seen his share of happiness and success, surely, but also suffering. As mentioned earlier, his childhood was far from ideal. And he has never shied away from the pain and sorrow of others. In fact, some of his most well-known Precious Moments figures were inspired by painful experiences shared with him by acquaintances and friends. For example, in 1990, a close friend of his named Jean Besett was dying of cancer. On one of his visits to her in the hospital, she said that she felt that God was standing beside her through this misery. Sam immediately started work on a new figurine, rushing its production in order to present it to her before she died. It was a small child sleeping in a hospital bed while another child angel stood by. The caption read, "He stands beside me."

Indeed, 1990 was a very painful year for Sam. Not only did he lose a close friend, but he lost his son, Philip, who died in an auto accident. He was twenty-seven, married, and left behind two children. Sam was utterly devastated. Not long after Philip's death, Sam and Katie were separated, and later divorced.

After Philip's funeral, at a loss for meaningful words or theological answers, he felt a burning need to create something to express his pain. The result was the now famous figure of an angel in a cute little convertible driving up to a blond boy hitchhiking on the side of the road. The license plate on the car says, HEAVEN BOUND. The angel tilts her head slightly to read a sign the boy is holding up. Written in an awkward kindergarten script, it says, GOING HOME.

By all accounts I've seen, there is not a pernicious or sarcastic bone in Sam's body. All who have met him describe him as a warm, deeply emotional, and sympathetic human being. He is a feeler. He listens to other people's stories, especially the sad ones, and often responds by creating something that might offer some kind of comfort without glossing over the pain.

For those of us who are not big Precious Moments fans, it's hard to see how Precious Moments figures could speak to pain without glossing it over, sugarcoating it in sweetness, making it "just precious." For me, it took a visit to the symbolic center of Sam's precious universe, Precious Moments Chapel, perched on a grassy hillside southwestern Missouri near the old town of Carthage, to get it.

Michelangelo and Butcher

The genesis of Precious Moments Chapel is well known among Precious Moments enthusiasts, who seem to know as much about Sam's life as they do about his figures.

By the early 1980s, Sam's newfound prosperity had led to a desire to express his thankfulness to all those who loved his work. Awed by a visit to the Sistine Chapel in Rome, he wondered whether he might find an opportunity to create his own chapel, which might glorify God and host similar religious experiences in others.

It was 1984, and he had made a trip to Arizona on business. Instead of returning home to Michigan by plane, he decided to rent a car and drive so that he could be open to God leading him to the right location to begin building the chapel of his dreams. Adding a certain element of asceticism to this vision-quest story, it is said that he did not get off the highway except to take care of his most basic needs. Road weary after about four days of traveling, he passed the exit for Highway HH off State Highway 71 outside Carthage, Missouri, and felt called to look there. He spent the night in nearby Joplin, and the next morning found a realtor to show him property in the Carthage area. He immediately found what he had been looking for, a seventeen-and-a-half-acre lot with an old stone farmhouse a few miles south of Highway HH. This was the place. He purchased it the same day. Soon he and his family had moved there. Chapel construction began about a year later, in 1985, and by 1989 it was open to visitors.

A visitor's center and buffet restaurant were also built, and soon Precious Moments Chapel had become a pilgrimage destination for hundreds of thousands of Precious Moments devotees. Over the years Sam annexed many more acres and added other attractions, most notably a Victorian "Wedding Island" complete with storybook house and chapel surrounded by a forty-acre man-made lake, and the Fountain of Angels. Today, Precious Moments Inspiration Park draws more than 400,000 visitors per year.

Inspiration Park

My daughter, Sophie, and I visited the park for two days in June of 2004. Like many Precious Moments pilgrims, we flew into Tulsa, Oklahoma, and drove a hundred miles north, through Cherokee country, into the grassy rolling pastures and farmlands of southwest Missouri. We stayed outside the historic town of Carthage at the Best Western Precious Moments Hotel, a hotel like most other Best Westerns but for its dusty pink walls and pervasive Precious Moments memorabilia. Owned and operated by the Precious Moments Inspiration Park, which is just a few miles away, the hotel fills up on most weekends. The check-in line at the reception desk included a pair of elderly women, two older married couples, and a woman and her ten-year-old daughter with matching outfits (Sophie whispered to me that they were also wearing matching makeup). Through conversations with the reception desk and complimentary breakfast bar personnel, we learned that the majority of their guests are elderly couples, many of whom come in larger groups. Many stay for several days, even weeks.

"The women go to Precious Moments every day," one young woman explained, "to see the chapel, to shop, and just to visit with their friends. The men either hang around here or go golfing." (Hotel brochures advertise a package deal that includes passes to both Precious Moments Inspiration Park and the nearby golf course.) "But now that school's out," she added, "we're seeing more and more kids, especially mother-daughter pairs." I think we may have been the only father-daughter pair, but I didn't ask.

It's almost impossible to get lost on the drive from the hotel to the park, thanks to the best signage I think I've ever seen. There's only one turn, onto Chapel Road from Highway HH, and every half mile or so there's a large billboard with a smiling Precious Moments face assuring visitors that they're on the right track and letting them know how much farther they have to go. As they approach the park, the signage frequency increases, with arrows pointing drivers to the main parking lot of the visitor's center and other sites. All of this is very comforting. It instills trust. We can rely on our good hosts at Precious Moments.

There are two large parking lots near the visitor's center, with lots of room for buses. When we arrived, on a Tuesday around midday, we counted well over a hundred cars. By the end of the day, that number had nearly doubled. On weekends, we were told, both lots fill up with cars and buses.

In front of the visitor's center there is a courtyard with an elaborate bronze fountain sculpture, somewhat reminiscent of Trevi Fountain in Rome but for the fact that all the figures, while Romanesque in posture and draped attire, were distinctly, how do I say it, Precious?

Inside the visitor's center is a reception area with maps and other orienting information, a huge gift shop, a hands-on exhibit of the making of the porcelain bisque figures, and a virtual town of medieval stone building facades and castle turrets—much like the "It's a Small World" set at Disney World—populated by mechanical Precious Moments figures going about their happy, innocent business. Inside one window, several of them are practicing formal dance steps. Inside another is a boy painting (Sam Butcher? It's hard to tell. Precious Moments figures don't exactly resemble those they represent, except by way of what they're doing.) A boy on a roof is flying a kite. At the other end of his string an angel, only one of her mechanical wings flapping, is holding his kite.

Although there was a certain Disneyesque quality to some of the park's features and in its meticulously clean neatness, Sophie and I noticed a very different ethos among the visitors. We saw none of the dull, over-saturated, expressionless faces so common among Orlando tourists. No one passed us and made eye contact without smiling and saying hello. Granted, this is the Midwest, where people actually do smile and say hello to strangers, even in a mall or airport or IHOP. But it was clear that people were especially happy to be here, and assumed that they shared that happiness with other visitors.

Precious Moments staff members, distinguishable by name tags and deep blue polo shirts, were very friendly, knowledgeable, and always happy to answer questions. I talked with many of them, from shuttle-bus drivers to receptionists to tour guides to restaurant servers. Most had worked there for at least five years, and to a person they said they loved their jobs. And that they loved Sam Butcher. Although he rarely visits the park these days, they all have warm recollections of interactions with him and are quick to tell stories of his generosity and his interest in and compassion for others. Brittany, a bubbly African-American woman who has worked in Sam's Buffet restaurant for eleven years, couldn't say enough positive things about the park and Sam.

"Brittany's famous!" another restaurant server interrupted while Sophie and I were talking with her next to the fountain drinks. "There's a Precious Moments doll modeled on her!" Brittany gave a modest smile. Later, in the gift shop, I found the Brittany doll, a limited edition light-brown figure with curly hair parted on the side and a calico dress of green, pink, and white. Created in 1998 and retired in 2000, it continues to be a very popular doll for collectors.

For Brittany, as for other staff members, whether or not Sam has modeled a doll on them, the park is not only a good job but a meaningful place of work. Their work feels purposeful to them. "The people are mostly just great," Brittany told us. "Some of them can be a little cranky when they get off the bus after a long hot ride, but even those ones get over it quickly. They feel moved by this place. They come here for peace, and for healing. It's nice to be part of a place like that."

There are two main attractions, one to the south of the visitor's center and one to the north. To the south is the Fountain of Angels, where two elaborate musicals show each day: the "Springs of Living Water" show in the afternoon, and the 9/11-inspired "Everlasting Promise" show in the morning. The publicity literature and recorded introduction before each show emphasize size and volume, aiming to set up visitors for an experience of religious awe in the face of sublime bigness. Housed in a one-hundred-foot-high enclosure with stadium seating, the fountain is a massive four-tier structure including more than three hundred bronze Precious Moments figures, all designed and sculpted by Sam Butcher himself. There are 265 nozzles. The water reservoir holds 109,000 gallons. During a show, the fountain pumps 16,000 gallons of water per minute through five miles of piping.

Sophie and I beheld the "Springs of Living Water" show. It consists of a carefully choreographed dance of fountain streams and bursts, synchronized with gospel songs sung by small choirs (much like those typical of televangelism shows). Huge plumes of water resembling candelabras and cathedral arches, illuminated by colored spotlights, shoot forth from cute Precious Moments figures. The central geyser reaches seventy-five feet in the air. The literature says that it represents "our relationship with God." The theme of all the songs, consistent with the emphasis on size and volume, is the glory and grandeur of God. The grand finale consists of a film projected onto a sixty-foot screen of mist sprayed across the background of the fountain sculptures. First, we saw an image of the Precious Moments Chapel. Then Jesus, with long flowing brown hair and a beard, dressed in white robes, appeared in the distance, near the chapel door, and began walking toward us. As the music rose to a crescendo, he spread out his hands in a gesture of grace and welcome (though, as Sophie noted, it also looked like he was directing the music).

After the show, the two hundred or so audience members were allowed to leave the seating area and take a closer look at the fountain itself. Almost all of them did so, many lingering there for more than a half hour, posing for pictures and admiring the handy work.

Although awesome grandeur is clearly the emphasis of this show, I was intrigued to discover that its inspiration, as with other Precious Moments works, was suffering. According the recorded introduction at the beginning of the show, Sam Butcher began creating the Fountain of Angels during a time of severe depression related to difficulties in his own life. What those difficulties were, the voice doesn't say, but it might have had to do with continuing grief over his son's death and his separation and divorce from his wife, Katie, which happened around that time. In any case, during his time of suffering and sadness, a scripture passage came to him from Psalm 42: "As the hart [or deer] panteth after the water brooks, so panteth my soul after thee, O God. My soul thirsteth for God, for the living God: when shall I come and appear before God? My tears have been my meat day and night, while they continually say unto me, Where is thy God?" This is a "lament Psalm," one of the biblical Psalms that gives voice to suffering and the experience of the absence of God, often in very disarming ways. For Sam Butcher, it gave voice to his experience of suffering and his longing for divine presence in the midst of it. According to the recorded introduction, moreover, he realized that water had always been a powerful image of God for him. Soon he began designing and creating the Fountain of Angels, which opened in 1997.

Going to the Chapel

The Fountain of Angels may be the park's most spectacular attraction, but its sacred center is Precious Moments Chapel. Perched on a low grassy hill overlooking a valley behind the visitor's center and surrounded by well-manicured paths, gardens, fountains, and sculptures (many dedicated to the memory of people who have died), the pink and peach stucco chapel is built like a modern cathedral. Its tall, steep-roofed main building is flanked on either side by smaller wings whose lines resemble flying buttresses. An archway in the center leads to the door, which is made of wood imported from the Philippines and hand-carved by Sam. On the face of each wing is a bronze façade shaped like an arched window. The one on the left depicts an Old Testament scene in signature Butcher style: a Precious Moses carries the two tablets of the Ten Commandments down a

Precious Moments Chapel

stairway from the heavens to meet a Precious Moments Israelite family (the father wears a yarmulke) waiting below. The one on the right depicts a New Testament scene in which a Precious Jesus preaches while an angel in the clouds above him holds a large cross. These, then, depict what many evangelical Christians would call the Old Covenant (i.e., the Law of Moses) and the New Covenant (i.e., the Gospel of Christ), each precious in its own way.

Guided tours of the chapel are given, free of charge, on the hour throughout the day. Our tour, early on a Wednesday morning before the tour buses had arrived, included about twenty people. Along with the two of us there were four families with small children and a group of older women traveling together. We came from Kentucky, Ohio, New Jersey, Georgia, Florida, and California. Our guide, a friendly and soft-spoken woman named Pat, was extremely knowledgeable about every detail of the chapel. It was clear that she had a genuine love for this place and the stories about Sam's work on it, and that she was eager to share that love with others.

The central cathedral space is about twenty-five feet wide, fifty feet long, and just over thirty feet high. Having heard that this space was inspired by the Sistine Chapel, I was hoping to find a Precious Moments version of Michelangelo's depiction of the creation of Adam: a muscular, white-bearded Precious Moments figure reaching down from the heavens to touch the fingertips of another, younger figure created in his image. Alas.

Like the Sistine, however, the entire interior of Precious Moments Chapel is covered with paintings of biblical scenes. Consistent with the two bronze panels outside, the left wall of the chapel focuses on the Old Testament while the right wall focuses on the New Testament. Each side has four rows of paintings. On the Old Testament side, the highest row depicts Precious Moments angels; the second row depicts Sam's favorite biblical stories (including the prophetess and warrior-judge Deborah, here more precious than I imagined her when I read the book of Judges); the third row depicts biblical heroes (including Hannah and her son Samuel, and Esther); and the bottom row depicts aspects of service and kindness. The New Testament side follows the same pattern, except that the high-

est row depicts Jesus's disciples, then the life of Jesus, then the parables, and then a series of four paintings of Sam's grandchildren playing together on an island in each of the four seasons. Pat drew our
attention to what she said is nearly everyone's favorite disciple at the
top: the former tax collector, Matthew, here shown as a little boy
clutching an Internal Revenue Service manual.

On the back wall, above a choir loft, are seven more paintings
representing the seven days of creation. On day one, "let there be
light," we see three cute angels (or is that the Holy Trinity?), one
brown and two pink, lighting up a cloudy sky with flashlights. By day
seven, God's Sabbath, Adam and Eve are bathing near a waterfall
while horses and deer look on from a distance.

The high ceiling is covered with Precious Moments angels (I got
dizzy and lost count at sixty-something) playing among puffy clouds
and blue sky. One of them is unfinished. Pat told us that Sam only
noticed it the morning after he had spent a very long and difficult
day painting angels while lying on his back on scaffolding. He decided to leave it unfinished. I gather that he left it that way, then, to
remember that time of exhaustion and discouragement. That, too,
was a precious moment.

The clear center of attention in the chapel space is the large
mural on the front wall, presenting Sam's highly personal vision of
life after death in heaven. In an expansive Roman forum-like space
with large columns, fountains, and trees, dozens of Precious Moments angels and children play games and talk with one another.
Some are in the clouds or on a rainbow that arches across the top of
the picture. It's a very bright and busy place. Toward the front, at
eye-level, is an entrance area. Three angels (the same three in the
"let there be light" painting?) form a welcoming committee: one
holds a sign, upside down, with the word WELCOME written on it, and
the other two hold another sign on which they've written TO YOUR

Front Mural, Precious Moments Chapel

HEAVENLY HOME. A little girl in a red dress is about to step through a gold gate, on which is written NO MORE TEARS, as other angels look on attentively. Behind the welcoming committee, a mother and father watch their diapered baby crawl toward them. Nearby, a little boy holds up a large red heart, torn in two, while an angel tapes it back together. Farther back, on a wide stairway, are children dressed as American soldiers.

Above the soldiers, at the top of the stairs, Pat pointed out another group gathered around the only one in all of heaven who is not a Precious Moments figure. Squinting slightly, we can see that it's Jesus, here depicted with long brown hair and beard in the style made popular by Warner Sallman's famous 1940 painting. Pat then pointed out where he is located in the picture space: dead center. Although Sam had not consciously intended to do so, he had placed Jesus in the very center of the painting.

Be that as it may, I don't think that this painting is centrally about Jesus, and I doubt anyone else would. What is most striking here is its depiction of those who have died. Many of whom, moreover, appear to have suffered considerably in life. "No more tears," the entrance gate reads. Angels patch broken hearts. Parents see their babies returned to them.

As Pat told us more about the mural, this sense of poignancy grew. "Most of the figures here are real people," she said. That is, they are images of people who have died and are now in heaven. In some cases, they are people Sam knew personally—his father, for example, who had been an auto mechanic, driving a little red race car along the rainbow. But many others are people whose sad stories he remembered or heard while painting the mural: a daughter who died at age twenty-one, weighing only fifty pounds, "who never walked or talked," now happily whole; a girl who died young after a terrible illness (I think she's the one in the red dress near the gate); another boy, Bradley, here depicted enjoying his favorite sport, tossing a basketball into a hoop held by an angel in a cloud; a girl named Shirley having a tea party (in this life, she had collected teapots).

Though I wouldn't call it majestic, it seems to me that Sam Butcher's mural is a remarkable work of ministry. It represents many pastoral relationships, in which he listened to the stories of suffering and loss, allowed the pain of survivors to be voiced, and then responded by creating for them an image of grace and redemption, beyond the tears of suffering and sting of death. In a very simple and unassuming way, he has helped them in their very real work of mourning as they try to integrate the traumas of suffering and loss into their lives in meaningful ways.

Philip's Room

Sam has said that his own experiences of pain and loss and his own struggles with depression have opened him to similar experiences of others. He has room in his heart, so to speak, for the suffering of others because he has made room for honest reflection on his own suffering. So too, I learned, with regard to the space of Precious Moments Chapel itself. Here the space Sam has devoted to creative work of mourning on behalf of the losses of others is in close physical proximity to the space he has devoted to his own loss.

In fact, the two spaces share the same wall. On the other side of the mural, annexed to the main chapel, we find a smaller chapel called Philip's Prayer Room, created by Sam in remembrance of his son, Philip, who, I mentioned earlier, died in a car accident in 1990. About twelve feet wide and thirty feet long with six rows of narrow pews, its focal point is another mural on the front wall showing a group of teary children standing around an empty bed in a boy's bedroom. Above the bed, in puffy clouds, three angels welcome a young boy into heaven. One is carrying a box of toys—the same toys that are in the bedroom—while two others are holding a sign that says, WELCOME HOME PHILIP. Two other angels look down from the clouds with concern at the children surrounding the empty bed.

In the back of the room is a glass case containing various memorabilia from Philip's life, including photos of him as an adult. As Sophie looked at a photo of him and his wife and kids walking on a beach, it suddenly dawned on her that he had not died as a child.

"You mean he was a *grown-up* when he died?" she whisper-shouted incredulously, clearly disturbed as she tried to put this fact together with the mural painting of a little boy going to heaven with a box of toys.

Her reaction is certainly understandable. Surely the mural is an unusual representation of the loss of an adult child. On the other hand, every figure in the world of Precious Moments is a child—from the Oklahoma City firefighter to Moses with the Ten Commandments. Every figure except the Jesus in the main chapel mural, anyway, and he seems very out of place, even up there in heaven. Beyond that, moreover, I think this mural speaks to the experiences of many parents who have lost grown children. I let myself imagine for a moment how I would grieve for Sophie if she were to die in her twenties. I do wonder whether my own recollected image of her, once lost, would often be as a six-year-old child. That, too, would probably be a disturbing thought for Sophie, so I kept it to myself.

Brochures and plaques in the Philip's Prayer Room make clear that this room is meant to host the experiences of others as well. It's not just a private memorial to Philip. The intention here is to create a space for others who have also lost children. In a note from Sam printed in a brochure called "Words of Comfort from Philip's Room," he writes that painting this mural was his own work of mourning when words failed him, and he expresses his hope that it will help others do the same:

> It was my way of working through the heartache that one feels for the loss of a loved one. When I was unable to express my feelings and could not talk to anyone, I came here

Front Mural, Philip's Prayer Room

to paint my emotions while I prayed that in some way the Lord would turn my sorrow into a concern for others who hurt as I did. As a parent, I know what it means to have lost a child; as a son I know what it means to lose a mother and father; as a friend, I understand your pain as well. If you came here today with a heavy heart, it is my prayer that you will find the peace and serenity that I feel whenever I enter this room.

I found this eloquently pastoral, transforming his story of loss, crisis, and creative grief work into a gesture of hospitality. The place of his work of mourning here becomes a place to host the same in others.

Books of Remembrance

This kind of hospitality—creating a space for others to give voice to their loss and to find comfort and healing in and through it—is perhaps most intentionally expressed in another small room, just around the corner from Philip's, explicitly designed to host others who are grieving lost loved ones.

On one wall of this room is a large glass case displaying numerous photos of people who have died, most of them children, smiling and laughing and playing with siblings and parents and friends. Around the room, on tables along the walls, are seven large white books, each laid open like a guest book at a wedding or funeral. But they're not exactly guest books. They're Books of Remembrance, in which Precious Moments Chapel visitors write whatever they want in remembrance of loved ones who have died. As I read several of the entries, I realized that most of them were not written *about* the dearly departed, but rather *to* them, almost like prayers. "We really miss you. We're getting along without you, but it's hard. You'd be so proud of . . . he's really helping out a lot."

Each of the seven books had about three hundred pages with six spaces per page, and each book had many pages already filled. At the front of each book a note indicated the date when it had been set out. Flipping to the beginning of one of the books, which had about one hundred pages filled (that is, about six hundred entries), I found that it had been out for about three weeks. Hundreds of visitors to the chapel were leaving messages and remembrances every day.

When Sophie and I entered the room, we hadn't noticed Cindy, a warm and friendly woman in her fifties, working away in the back corner. Quieter and less conspicuous than any librarian or cathedral abbess, she was carefully labeling several of the big white Books of Remembrance and shelving them in a wooden case designed specifically to hold them. She explained in a hushed voice that they had started leaving these books out for people to write their own notes in memory of or to lost loved ones back in 1995. Over the years, she told us, more and more visitors have come to write in them. She told us that there were sixty-nine of the books already labeled and shelved. (You can do the math.)

"Do you ever read the entries?" I asked.

"Sometimes I do. It's very touching. And it gets me back to what this place is really all about. It's a place of healing. It touches people deeply. It puts them in touch with their own experiences of loss. This isn't just a job. It's a ministry."

Indeed, as I watched Cindy ever so carefully and reverently handling these books, enshrining them in a specially made case, it occurred to me that her role here was much like that of Sam himself. Sam took the stories of other people's sadness and loss and sanctified them by painting them into the mural. Cindy takes the words of loss and grief and remembrance from the books and sanctifies them by creating for them a special, revered place in the chapel. That is indeed a ministry.

Just Precious

As Sophie and I left the chapel, a familiar old-time gospel song was being piped through the surrounding gardens through little outdoor speakers nestled among shrubs and Precious Moments sculptures.

"Come home, come home," the soothing woman's voice sang, "Ye who are weary, come home."

As Cindy reminded us, many who come to Precious Moments Chapel are indeed weary, weary enough to break down and confess it, to give voice to it or to confess it in a book, and to seek comfort. Sam Butcher and his staff have managed to create a place that is not only open to such confessions and such desires for comfort, but that in fact welcomes them, to such an extent that people who come to Precious Moments Chapel know that they are coming for this reason.

I had come to Precious Moments Chapel not weary and heavy burdened but nonetheless curious. I'd read a lot about the place—about the Sistine-inspired chapel paintings and murals, and about Philip's Prayer Room with its representations of Philip as a small boy, despite the fact that he had died as an adult. From a distance, it all seemed like a strange mix of creepiness and sappiness. I expected that it would be hard to keep my powers of wry observation and ideological criticism, limited though they may be, in check. I was wrong. The place completely disarmed me with its simple, honest, precious expression of childlike suffering, loss, and hope for healing.

Intellectual culture (in which I'm an increasingly disaffected in-terloper) likes to tell itself a well-rehearsed narrative of personal and societal development. It begins with childlike innocence, simplicity, and naive faith and ends with mature knowledge, complexity, and sophisticated skepticism. As knowledge increases, faith diminishes. The more we know, the less we believe. On a larger social-historical scale, the more a society develops, the less it needs religion, which will eventually become irrelevant, a relic of our childish past. In some ways, this narrative is a modern Western version of the biblical myth of the fall: having partaken of the Tree of Knowledge, we must leave Eden, that garden of childhood delights in which we com-muned with one another and with God. It may be painful, but it's also necessary and even inevitable. Faith, then, for societies as for individuals, is equated with intellectual simplicity that diminishes in the course of gaining knowledge through education and research.

I suspect that there are several reasons why we like this story as a way of understanding our personal and social histories. First, it makes pretty good sense of our experience. How many of us, after all, associate our loss of childhood faiths (all kinds) with revelations that came to us from reading, study, experiment, and other learning experiences? ("I lost my faith when I read Nietzsche.") Second, this story justifies that loss: in it we tell ourselves that it was necessary to lose faith in order to advance in knowledge. Third, it reinforces a class system in our society, distancing intellectual elites from others with different kinds of education and experience. Fourth, I suspect that it provides us with protection from those simple childlike inklings of faith, those glimmers of hope, which still dwell within us, however latently, and terrify us. Terrify because they make us vulnerable to disappointment (again?). And because they suggest that maybe we haven't come as far as we'd like to think.

In some respects, Precious Moments confirms this story, especially in its equation of faith, simplicity, and childhood, all of which it idealizes. And yet in other respects, Precious Moments does not maintain the equation, because it's not that simple. Faith and childhood are clearly idealized here. I'd go so far as to suggest that they are consecrated as the privileged form of expression, especially for expressing suffering and loss. But is it right to equate these with simplicity? Why do I equate complexity of expression with complexity of life experience and religious response? Why do I think that a simple expression expresses a simple experience?

Isn't it just precious? No, not just. In the course of my visit, I came to believe that the appearance of simplicity here is superficial, a precious sugar coating over an abyss of feeling so deep and complex that it cannot be adequately expressed. "When I was unable to express my feelings and could not talk to anyone, I came here to paint my emotions. . . ." It is this depth of feeling, churning beneath the pastel surfaces, that speaks to visitors of Precious Moments Chapel in sighs too deep for words.

Chapter Eight

MR. BROWN'S CABINET
OF PRAYERS

Don Brown Rosary Collection
Skamania County, Washington

Waterfalls and rocks tumble down mountainsides blanketed with evergreens and into the massive Columbia River, which slowly rolls along between western Oregon and Washington. The snowy peaks of Mount Adams, Mount Hood, and Mount St. Helens look on the river from a distance. Eagles, hawks, and falcons fly overhead. Bear, deer, elk, and coyotes roam the thick woods. Old wooden log flumes, no longer in use, run along the mountainsides, skeletons of a rapidly passing industry. The banners of the latest Columbia Gorge industry, outdoor recreation, would have to be the brightly colored sails and kites of the thousands of wind surfers who flock to the river bend near Hood River, Oregon, about fifty miles upstream from the city of Portland. Many claim that this part of the river has the best wind-surfing wind in the world.

The Columbia Gorge is a familiar area for me. I was born in Hood River, and I spent my early childhood years in the Forest Service ranger district town of Wind River, on the Washington side. I remember when the *Lassie* television crew came to town to film an episode in which Lassie dove through a sugar glass window in my neighbor's house. After shooting the scene, my dad, a real forest ranger, had his picture taken with Lassie and Ranger Cory. I remember watching the gold-red glow of massive forest fires on distant horizons, knowing my dad was out there, and running to the Wind River dam to watch helicopters scoop water into their huge hanging buckets and carry it off to dump on the blaze.

When my dad retired from the Forest Service in Minnesota, he and my mom immediately moved back to the area, making their home about halfway up Wind Mountain, a traditional Native American vision-quest site. Looking down the gorge from their deck you can see the massive landslide known in Klickitat Indian legend as The Bridge of the Gods. One story tells of two brothers separated by the great river. The Great Spirit built a land bridge to reconnect them. When they and their peoples began to fight, the Spirit destroyed the bridge, leaving a large land mass reaching only part way across the river. The Cascade Rapids, which were created by this narrowing of the river, were one of the most treacherous parts of the Oregon Trail. Since 1926 there has been a modern toll bridge spanning the river at the same place. Beyond the Bridge of the Gods, just out of view, is Bonneville Dam, built by new gods of great power.

A couple miles north of the Bridge of the Gods, at the base of Table Mountain, is Stevenson, Washington, the seat of Skamania County. On the west end of town, at the base of Table Mountain, is the spectacular new Columbia Gorge Interpretive Center Museum. Established in 1995 along with the Dolce Skamania Lodge, the Museum's mission is to preserve and share the history of Skamania County and the Columbia River Gorge. During one of my visits to my folks' place while dad was going through his miserable decline with Lou Gehrig's, they told me about the museum's most unusual attraction: "the world's largest rosary collection." Which just goes to show that home, no matter how familiar, is full of surprises.

Sitting close to the river, the museum building combines drab gray concrete with large blond rough-hewn logs and timbers, recalling the interaction of wilderness and industry that so characterizes the last two centuries of gorge history. The interior of the museum, designed by Jean Jacques André, consists of several exhibits, each independent from and interrelated to the others. On the ground floor, the First Peoples exhibit is connected to a collection of artifacts from early gorge industries by a small stream that runs through them all. On one side of the stream, standing on a wooden perch attached to a shale cliff, is a statue of a young Native American man dipping a small fish net into the water. On the other side is a two-story-high life-size replica of a late-nineteenth-century water-powered machine called a fishwheel, designed to scoop thousands of salmon per day during their annual spawning runs up the river. Across the room, downstream, is a massive black 1907 Corliss Steam Engine used by Wind River Lumber Company to saw and convey giant logs. Next to it is a 1921 Mack log truck, and overhead is an airplane from the ninth Aero Squadron. All around the main space are smaller exhibits focusing on particular aspects of history and early life in the gorge. Emanating from the First Peoples exhibit and reaching throughout the museum space, visitors hear a recording of Native American children from the Wishram tribe chanting in their native Upper Chinook language. The overall effect of the museum space is to fold together periods and cultures in a way that maintains the distinctness of each element of the gorge's cultural history while recognizing the complex ways in which they implicate one another, sometimes tragically.

The Rosary Collection

Upstairs is a half-floor that overlooks the fishwheel, the Native American fisherman, and the steam engine. A sign on the main wall, just past a small theater, reads, SPIRITUAL QUEST. Listening to the Wishram chants rising from the First Peoples exhibit below, the phrase brings to mind the Native American tradition of the vision quest, a rite of passage in which a young person goes alone into the wilderness seeking a dream vision in which she or he receives a protective spirit.

But the architecture of the space near the Spiritual Quest sign is not exactly Native American. Indeed, it is distinctly Roman Catholic, albeit with a Pacific Northwest flavor: a series of five blond wooden archways that form a narrow, cathedralesque space. At the far end, elegantly displayed, is a collection of ritual furniture and objects taken from Roman Catholic churches: a mid-nineteenth-century altar from St. James Mission Church in nearby McMinneville, Oregon; a statue of Saint Dominic from Rome; a sanctuary lamp from the original St. James Church at Fort Vancouver; a kneeling bench, or *pre dieu* (before God), which was once used by the first archbishop of the Oregon Territory; and a small, ornately decorated display case containing speck-size relics of Saints, among them Benedict, Claudia, Ursula, and Clara.

As I approached the opening of the hall, the Wishram chants rising from below were gradually overcome by other voices, again distinctly Roman Catholic, emanating from the altar space: a choir singing the traditional Dominican chant.

Taken together, the worshipful chant music, the low lighting, the archways, and the orientation toward the altar at the far end mark the area off as Roman Catholic sacred space.

Lining the arched hallway on both sides are vertical glass cases that hold the more than 4,000 rosaries of the Don Brown Rosary Collection. Each case contains hundreds of rosaries draped neatly on hooks. Some are tiny, with beads the size of pinheads. Some are ring rosaries, meant to wear around one's finger. Most are about two feet

Don Brown Rosary Collection

long, made to wear around the neck. Some are larger, made to wear around the waist of a monk's or nun's habit. The largest one in the collection, sixteen feet long, hangs on a wall at the far end of the cases.

No two rosaries in the collection are the same. Each is unique. There are beads of every imaginable color and shape, made from almost every imaginable material—bone, wood, ceramic, stone, metal, shell, seed, nut, and even, on the sixteen footer, Styrofoam balls (a note explains that it was made by school children in Massachusetts for a play). The crosses attached to the rosaries are just as widely varied in size, shape, and material. The most striking are those sporting gamma crosses, or swastikas. Before it was co-opted and forever stigmatized by the Nazis, it was a popular symbol for the Christian Cross, and long before that it was a South Asian symbol of well-being. Other objects are also attached to many of the rosaries. One has small hand-carved ivory rabbits interspersed between the beads. Another has a hand-carved skull dangling from it. Another has several medallions with images of Egyptian gods.

One small black cocoa-beaded rosary is displayed prominently in its own case along with five bronze medallions—three of President John Fitzgerald Kennedy, one of the Madonna holding baby Jesus, and one of Pope Pius XI. According to the tour brochure, this rosary was the one John Fitzgerald Kennedy used during his service in World War II. He donated it to the collection in 1960, shortly after he announced he would be running for president.

Like prayer beads used in numerous other religious traditions, from Buddhism to Islam, Catholic rosaries are concentration and memory devices designed to facilitate prayer and meditation. In specifically Catholic terms, they facilitate devotional meditation on the mysteries of Jesus's life, death, and Resurrection.

Although prayer beads had been used since at least the eleventh century to help keep count of psalm recitations, Hail Marys, and Our Fathers, the institution of the rosary as a recommended form of Catholic devotion is traditionally ascribed to St. Dominic (1170–1221), who is said to have been instructed by Our Lady to preach its practice as an antidote to heresy and sin. Over time, there developed a complex system for praying the rosary that continues to this day. The one hundred and fifty beads are divided into fifteen sets of ten, or decades. For each decade, the one praying offers Hail Mary prayers while meditating on one of the Fifteen Mysteries of the Gospels (one Our Father prayer is offered between each decade). These Fifteen Mysteries are divided into three groups of five: the Joyful Mysteries, focusing on Mary's witness to and pondering of the birth and childhood of Jesus; the Sorrowful Mysteries, focusing on Jesus's agony in the Garden and his trial, torture, and death; and the Glorious Mysteries, focusing on Jesus's Resurrection, his ascension, and his sending of the Holy Spirit to be with his disciples, as well as Mary's assumption and coronation as Queen of Heaven and Earth. The rosary has developed as a work of religious art designed to facilitate personal devotional prayer.

Each of the rosaries in this collection, then, is a physical remnant of personal piety, its beads shined and darkened by the daily fingering of a devotee concentrating on the mysteries of her or his faith. As with prayer beads of other religious traditions, the rosary is a deeply personal religious object. Each represents the faith life of an individual, or perhaps generations of individuals through whom it has been passed. Each is what remains of countless prayers.

As I wandered among them, admiring the vast variety of color, shape, and size displayed within this very specific type of ritual object, I found myself overwhelmed. I felt as though the space were haunted by whispers of prayer. Standing in their midst, I could almost hear the quiet cacophony of hushed Hail Marys and clicking beads, smooth from thousands of prayerfully caressing fingers. It's almost too much to take in—thousands of personal, intimate artifacts of faith draped together like a hoard of treasure. After a few minutes of trying unsuccessfully to take in the collection as a whole, I felt the need to focus in on one rosary at a time and to learn its story.

The collection has been organized with this desire in mind. Attached to each rosary is a small paper tag, carefully turned toward the glass so that visitors can read its number. Between two of the glass cases is a computer terminal with directions for how to look specific rosaries up by number. The record for each rosary includes information concerning the age of the rosary, its composition, who donated it, and, when known, who used it. Here are a few examples of the many I read:

> *Rosary, fifteen decades, made of black cocoa beads. Sterling silver center connecting medal; genuine ebony and sterling silver cross. Donor: Rev. Benedictine Sisters of Clyde, Missouri.*

> *Rosary, five decades, made of black beads each containing a colored portrait of a different Madonna under isinglass, with the title in Latin on the reverse side corresponding to the Litany of the Blessed VIRGIN. Black composition centerpiece with a Madonna under isinglass, with earth from the Roman catacombs enclosed in the reverse side from where the rosary came. The rosary was acquired by Miss Anna Masuch of Minneapolis, during her Lourdes tour of 1958. Presented by Mrs. Anna Masuch at the Sanctuary of Our Sorrowfull Mother, Portland, Ore.*

Rosary, five decades, a rosary necklace as worn by the Past Faithful Navigator of the Order of the Knights of Columbus. Made of rich conical shaped crystal beads inlaid with red centers. Silver centerpiece with relief of the Sacred Heart of Jesus and Fourth Degree emblem on the reverse side. At the end is attached the official Badge of the Past Faithful Navigator.

Sometimes, the record includes fragments of the story behind the rosary, leaving visitors to fill in the blanks with their own narrative imaginations. My favorite was a rather large rosary necklace with beads made of Job's Tears, which are thumb-size, teardrop-shaped brown seeds frequently used for rosaries and chaplets. The nickel-clad ebony crucifix is damaged, the chain is rusty, and the whole rosary is inextricably tangled up with a driftwood branch. Reading the record, I learned that this rosary, which is about fifty years old, was found washed ashore on Leetonia Beach, Florida, by a nun, Sister Mary Michella, S.N.D., from Notre Dame College in South Euclid, Ohio, a suburb of Cleveland.

Mr. Brown

Just as each of the rosaries has a personal story behind it, so also does the collection itself. It is the story of Don Brown, a man instrumental in establishing and promoting the Skamania County Historical Society which owns and directs the museum. Indeed, these rosaries are his only material remains, and it is quite likely that this museum wouldn't be here at all if it weren't for Mr. Brown and his collection.

Donald A. Brown was born in 1895 in Tualatin, Oregon. He was not raised in a Catholic family. In fact, his fascination with rosaries came years before his adult conversion to Catholicism, during a long confinement with severe pneumonia in a nearby Catholic hospital.

"It was there that I saw the rosary being worn on the habits of the Sisters of Mercy," he wrote in the *Skamania County Pioneer* in his latter years. "While my love for sacred art seems to have been born with me, the rosary has always held a special fascination for me. I consider my former years of illness a special blessing since the rosary was the beginning of the faith of my adoption."

I find this a fascinating account. Was he attracted to the religious piety and devotional practice the sisters represented? Did he see them not only wearing but praying their rosaries? Or was he attracted to the visual and tactile beauty of the things themselves— or, for that matter, of the sisters who wore them and cared for him? Probably all of the above, and more. In any case, he emerged from his illness with an abiding absorption in the rosary, an object that must have in some way represented both his suffering and their care.

In 1917, while living in The Dalles, Oregon, he began collecting rosaries in earnest. In 1920 he moved to North Bonneville, Washington, to oversee a family tract of land. There he continued to build his collection, which he kept in a "rosary chapel" in his house, always happy to welcome visitors. Around the same time he converted to Catholicism and became a lay brother in the Third Order of the Dominicans—named for St. Dominic, Brown's patron saint, who, you'll recall, was an early promoter of the rosary.

By the 1950s his rosary collection was gaining attention from Catholics all over the world. He continued acquiring special rosaries through travels and correspondences (for example, John Fitzgerald Kennedy's rosary, which he requested upon hearing his announcement of candidacy for president). But as the collection's fame grew, many were sent to him unsolicited, as gifts, including rosaries used by Father Flanagan of Boys Town, Al Smith, the first Catholic to run for president (in 1928), Lawrence Welk, Robert Kennedy, and Dag Hammerskjold.

But the size and quality alone of Mr. Brown's rosary collection would not have been enough to land it in the museum. All the while he was collecting rosaries, he was also actively involved in establishing and promoting the Skamania County Historical Society, which he and his father helped found in 1926. In fact, it was in relation to this newly established society that he had taken his first crack at creating a roadside attraction: he built a life-size replica of the mid-nineteenth-century block house used by the Army at Fort Rains as a military post on the Oregon Trail. That project eventually fell apart—literally—due to neglect. But the rosary collection didn't. In fact, it became the strategic means for Mr. Brown and the Skamania County Historical Society to establish a museum to preserve and share the history of the area.

When the town of North Bonneville was purchased by the Army Corps of Engineers in order to add a second powerhouse for the dam, Mr. Brown lost his family property and began searching for another home for the collection. His requirements for donating the collection were that it never be divided or sold in parts, and that it remain on display in perpetuity for the people of Skamania County. Early on, he approached The Grotto in Portland, a pilgrimage site built into and on top of a one-hundred-and-ten-foot basalt cliff that includes chapels, a rosary walkway, the Stations of the Cross, a grotto dedicated to Our Sorrowful Mother, and a monastery of the Servants of Mary. It seems like The Grotto would have been an ideal home for the collection, especially given its emphasis on Mary piety and its rosary walkway, which takes visitors through the Fifteen Mysteries of the rosary. Had they taken it, the Columbia Gorge Interpretive Center Museum might never have come to be. But The Grotto was unable to meet Mr. Brown's requirements.

In 1973, Skamania County accepted the collection and agreed to comply with Mr. Brown's requirements. It was given a home in the basement of the courthouse annex building in Stevenson. On Mr. Brown's recommendation, an exhibit of Native American artifacts was added in a separate room. So began the museum. Twenty-two years and a tremendous amount of fundraising and planning later, the Columbia Gorge Interpretive Center Museum opened, and the Don Brown Rosary Collection was given a place of prominence.

Sadly, Mr. Brown didn't live to see the new museum. In December 1978, while Christmas shopping in Eugene, Oregon, he was hit and killed by a car as he crossed the street in his wheelchair.

Sharon Tiffany, the executive director of the museum, worked with him from 1975 to 1978. She remembers him as a mild and friendly man with an abiding passion for rosaries. "Whether or not the conversation started with rosaries," she told me with a laugh, "it was sure to get there eventually!" A Baptist with little background in Catholic tradition, she was impressed by his passion to educate others about Catholicism and about the rosary. She also recalls how he would accompany visitors into the rosary collection and offer to pray the rosary with them. Sometimes someone would bring her or his own rosary in order to hold it along with one from the collection that had been specially blessed in hopes of transferring the blessing. Indeed, although that original room in the basement of the annex was fairly plain, it had an aura of sacred space that Mr. Brown worked to maintain. It was an intimate place of prayer. The design of the Don Brown Rosary Collection in the new museum reflects the desire to maintain that sense of sacred space, albeit in a higher-church, more cathedralesque way.

Cabinet of Prayers

In some respects, the Don Brown Rosary Collection is part of the centuries-old "cabinet of curiosities" tradition in which individuals would collect and display varieties of cultural and natural curiosities from around the world in an effort to represent the fullness of creation in all its messy diversity. Such collections were sometimes called *Wunderkammern*, "chambers" or "cabinets of wonder." Herein lies the prehistory of European zoos, museums, and gardens, not to mention the curio cabinets of heirlooms, rocks, butterflies, birds eggs, thimbles, and spoons that we find in many homes today.

While Mr. Brown's rosary collection is indeed an heir of this tradition, here the profuse messiness of the early cabinets of curiosities is replaced by a far more controlled profusion. Diversity is restricted to one particular kind of object, an object that is in fact both natural (in its material composition) and cultural (in its artifice and religious use). Moreover, for Mr. Brown, the objects in this collection were not merely curiosities or even wonders. For him, what began as a curiosity—something other, exotic, and as such fascinating to a young non-Catholic boy being cared for by rosary-wearing sisters —eventually became very familiar. In the beginning, the rosary was another world to him. But over time its fascinating otherness lured him out of his own familiar world. Over time it became his world.

For Mr. Brown, collecting rosaries became a calling, a form of religious devotion, even as the rosary itself is another form. Instead of a cabinet of wonders or curiosities, his is a cabinet of prayers.

Some might want to denigrate his collection as a form of fetishism. That would indeed be a curious charge from the perspective of the history of religion. For the concept of fetishism is closely linked to the modern Western prejudice against ritual objects, which it categorized as artifacts of primitive religion. The charge of fetishism, then, is inseparable from this modern Eurocentric disdain for the material, sensual aspects of religion, treating them as lower forms and privileging religions that are more purely reasonable, intellectual, doctrinaire. Like so many of the attitudes and values that shape modern Western thought, moreover, this disdain for material religious piety is an inheritance of Protestant religiosity, which has tended to define itself primarily over and against Catholicism.

I grew up in a Protestant context in which there was significant distrust of Catholic ritual practices, spaces, and objects. I'm embarrassed to think of it now, but I remember attending a Catholic church with my girlfriend in tenth grade, terrified that the sensual ritual elements of the service might seduce me away from right Christian doctrine, perhaps letting slip out an accidental Hail Mary or inadvertently paying allegiance to the Pope. As the priest dashed incense toward the congregation, I kept my head low, reading the Bible I had brought with me and praying that I might not be led astray. This may seem like an extreme case, but we can't underestimate the anti-Catholic prejudice built into much modern Protestant thought. Clearly it has diminished in recent years, especially as many conservative Protestants and Catholics have found common *moral* ground on which to stand in protest against liberal trends such as the ordination of women, reproductive rights, and interreligious dialogue, to name a few. Still, put a rosary in a conservative evangelical Protestant's hand and ask him to pray, and see if he doesn't quickly, if politely, hand it off as though it were unclean.

Later on, while attending a Christian (Free Methodist) college in Seattle, Washington, I grew increasingly fascinated with that which I had feared before. I began attending a high liturgy Episcopal cathedral on Capital Hill and eventually became a member. I was captivated by the aesthetics of worship there—the poetry of the prayer book, the grace of the ritual movements, the colors and smells and sounds. Worship there was a deeply sensual experience. There was theology too, but its mediation was at least as important as its message.

Along with a handful of other lapsed born-againers, I also grew fascinated by various forms of Roman Catholic and Orthodox monasticism and their traditional ritual practices and physical disciplines. These college friends and I would pass among us copies of the sayings of the desert fathers, lives of saints, and works describing ascetic practices, which we found particularly intriguing. Although none of us got to the point of wearing a hair shirt, we did fast regularly, and some of us created little prayer closets in our rooms.

Surely part of the attraction to high liturgy, monasticism, and other religious practices associated with Roman Catholic, Orthodox, and Episcopal traditions was their exotic allure. These traditions represented religious otherness to me, the tabooed "not-us" of my own upbringing. But part of their attraction was also due to a growing sense that my own inherited religious life was profoundly lacking in aesthetic experience. There had been too much emphasis on doctrinal theology. Too much headiness and not enough embodied experience. Although I couldn't have articulated it clearly then, I was coming to believe that religion without its smells and bells and beads is spiritually bankrupt.

Religious experience, no matter how lofty or self-transcending or ecstatic, is grounded in particular, embodied experiences of ritual practices that involve touching, seeing, hearing, smelling, tasting. Here again we encounter the paradox of the sacred. The transcendent is known in and through the immanent. I suspect that Mr. Brown understood this intuitively, even as a child sick with pneumonia at Mercy Hospital. *Pneuma* is Greek for breath, also spirit. In the New Testament, it's the word for divine spirit as well. Perhaps his severe pneumonia—a lung infection inhibiting him from breathing in, that is, from *inspiration*—was accompanied by a more spiritual pneumonia as well. In any case, the Sisters of Mercy cared for him in both body and spirit, and their rosaries stayed with him.

The Cabinet Makes the Man

In a 1594 speech transcribed and published as *Gesta Grayorum*, the philosopher Francis Bacon proposed that the marks of a princely gentleman should include (in addition to a library, a garden, and a "still-house" for scientific composition and experimentation) "a goodly huge cabinet" in which to collect wonders of nature and human creativity. The cabinet, Bacon suggests, makes the man.

Jean Jacques André, who designed the Don Brown Rosary Collection and the other exhibits in the museum, said that "artifacts often are the only physical evidence we have of someone's life." Sharing this view, Executive Director Sharon Tiffany leaned across the corner of her desk toward me and declared, "What you need to understand about the Don Brown Rosary Collection is that the reason it's here is because it *represents him*. He is a central figure in the history of Skamania County and the gorge. Without his work, the Skamania County Historical Society and this museum wouldn't be here. And this collection is pretty much all there is left of him." The museum, she explained, preserves and displays this collection as the tangible memory bank of Don Brown's life.

Bacon might well have approved. What better representation of the man than his cabinet? But Don Brown would no doubt have countered that the rosaries themselves don't so much represent him as they do the people who prayed them and treasured them before they came into his hands. They are made sacred by the devout touches and prayers of others that they bear.

Passing

I mentioned earlier that my parents first told me about the rosary collection. The first time I visited it, I went with them. At that time my dad, still in the relatively early stages of ALS, was strong enough to drive. The last time I visited, I drove myself, and on the way passed his grave on a grassy incline overlooking the Columbia River in the Stevenson Cemetery.

Dad left no rosaries behind. In fact, although he and mom have had many close Catholic friends in their adult life, he grew up in a Baptist church in Maine that was strongly prejudiced against and suspicious of Roman Catholicism. Some people in that church actually had wondered whether the Pope might be the Antichrist.

One day I will leave a rosary behind. It was given to me by one of Clover's workmates in an office job she had between college and seminary. Having heard that I was studying Hebrew Scriptures and Judaism and that I was interested in Catholic devotional practices, she bought it for me from a trip she took to Israel. It has small wooden beads and a small wooden cross wrapped in tin. In the center of the cross is a red glue dot containing a speck of Jerusalem soil. I try to pray with the rosary daily during the season of Lent, which in Christian tradition is a time of intense self-reflection in preparation for the celebration of Easter. The focus of Lent is on our mortality, following the story of Jesus as he moves toward the Cross. (On Ash Wednesday, which begins Lent, the minister says, "Remember that you are dust, and that to dust you shall return," as she draws a cross in ashes on your forehead.) I don't pray the Fifteen Mysteries with my rosary. I simply recite a single simple passage—like "as the hart longs for flowing streams, so my heart longs for you" (Psalm 42), or "the eye is not satisfied with seeing, nor is the ear filled with hearing" (Ecclesiastes 1), or, in Hebrew, "the breath of all of life blesses your name"—while meditating on particular people in my life whose situation is weighing on my mind. It's a way of bringing my own desires and the desires of others into convergence with God. For me, that's the power of prayer.

This past Lent, I prayed with my rosary for my mom. I think dad would have approved. I think Mr. Brown would have too.

Chapter Nine

ORA ET LABORA

Ave Maria Grotto
Cullman, Alabama

Nestled in rolling hills of pine, oak, and cedar just outside the small town of Cullman in the mountain lakes region of Alabama, about fifty miles north of Birmingham, are the old stone buildings and well-manicured gardens of St. Bernard Abbey. Founded in 1891 by Benedictine monks from St. Vincent's Abbey in Latrobe, Pennsylvania, to serve the religious needs of German Catholics in the area, the monastery now operates a successful preparatory high school and conference center. The mantra of the Benedictine monastic order is *ora et labora*, "pray and work," and the thirty or so monks of St. Bernard Abbey live it out daily, maintaining the one-hundred-sixty acres of grounds, operating the school and conference center, and helping in local parishes.

Today the abbey is best known not for its school or retreat center, as excellent as they are, but for its four-acre complex of miniature buildings and shrines called Ave Maria Grotto. Located on the hillside of what was once the quarry used by the monks to build the monastery's library and church, this tiny world unto itself includes well over a hundred shrines, mythological scenes, and replicas of famous buildings and pilgrimage destinations from throughout Europe, North and South America, Asia, and the Middle East.

The centerpiece of this two-block religious microcosmos is the

Ave Maria Grotto itself, a concrete cave structure measuring twenty-seven feet in height, depth, and width and dedicated to the Virgin Mary as Our Lady of Prompt Succor. *Grotto* is another word for *cave*, and some of the most well-known sacred grottos, which are typically consecrated by a miracle, are in fact natural caves. This one, of course, is a human creation. Yet it appears almost natural, its exterior overgrown with ivy and other green things, its mouth and interior lined with thousands of pieces of broken marble and other mineral-deposit-like shiny bits. Hanging from the ceiling are countless stalactites made of molded concrete and covered with broken pieces of colored glass and crushed stones.

Sheltered within this big thunder egg of a cave are three large Carrara marble statues, each weighing about a ton, set together atop an ornate altar frosted with glass dust. In the center is Mary, presented here as Our Lady of Prompt Succor, holding the baby Jesus, his hand extended toward visitors in a gesture of blessing. Flanking the holy couple are two figures kneeling in rapt adoration. On the left is St. Benedict, the fifth-century founder of the Benedictine monastic order, and on the right is Benedict's twin sister, St. Scholastica, founder of the Benedictine nuns.

Built into a hilly rock garden to the right of the grotto is an expansive complex of tiny, carefully labeled buildings and caves made of hand-molded concrete and decorated with small tiles, marbles, shells, and crushed stone. Five small tile signs planted among the rocks and ferns above this area announce the theme: SCENES... FROM...THE...HOLY...LAND...

In the middle of the area is the walled city of Jerusalem, complete with a most impressive replica of Herod's Temple. As with the other buildings here, the Temple is a delightful combination of exacting replication and creative ornamentation. On the one hand, from a few yards away, it appears to be a precise material representation of the Temple's structural features and proportions during the first century, before its destruction by the Romans in 70 CE, as depicted in many historical illustrations from textbooks. On the other hand, on closer scrutiny, nearly every square inch is creatively decorated with tiny found objects: blue, red, and turquoise marbles pressed into the concrete above windows and below rooflines, chicken-wire mesh above an arched doorway, shiny stones and shells decorating exterior walls and walkways. Here as throughout, both the realism and the ornamentation appear to have been carried out with enormous care.

Outside Jerusalem's walls are various buildings and spaces that represent scenes from biblical narrative and postbiblical Christian history. Three particular scenes serve to frame and orient this very large installation. First is the giving of the law in the wilderness of Sinai, represented by two tablets of the Ten Commandments placed above the city of Jerusalem. Between the two tablets stands a ten-inch-high wooden stick around which a black nail is twisted, depicting the Brazen Serpent, which had the power to save the Israelites from snakebite during the wilderness wanderings (believed by many to prefigure Christ). Second is the birth of Jesus, represented by a homestyle porcelain nativity set carefully arranged in the mouth of a ten-inch stone cave labeled "Bethlehem" to the left of the city. And third is the death and Resurrection of Jesus, represented by a miniature version of Golgotha and the empty tomb to the right of the city.

Other sites and structures outside the city walls include a three-inch-wide concrete and tile trail leading through overgrowths of ivy to Jacob's Well, encircled by tiny hand-formed bricks; St. Mary's Well at Nazareth, a foot-high arched alcove with a rusty half-inch pipe trickling holy water onto a floor covered with pennies, nickels, and dimes that have been tossed with prayers by adoring visitors; the

Herod's Temple, Scenes from the Holy Land, Ave Maria Grotto

Annunciation Church at Nazareth, its tower standing a few feet above the ferns growing around it, its walls built from finger-hewn brown stones and decorated with tiles of cream white and aqua blue; and the ruined home of Jesus's beloved partners in ministry, Mary and Martha, and the tomb of their brother, Lazarus (whom Jesus wept over before raising him from the dead), a small rock wall with an opening barely large enough to stick in a thumb.

As remarkable as the grotto and Scenes from the Holy Land are, the complex that attracts the most attention from visitors is nearby Rome. Just as Herod's Temple is the centerpiece of Jerusalem, the centerpiece of Rome is a replica of St. Peter's Basilica, the burial place of the church's first pope, the Apostle Peter. The main cathedral building, hand formed from concrete and neatly painted, has been decorated with pieces of tiles and miniature columns, all arranged for perfect symmetry. In front of the cathedral is a fairly accurate replica of the four-acre Vatican courtyard, encircled by a covered walkway whose roof is supported by about a hundred finger-size white columns.

Along the hillside of the old quarry area behind St. Peter's are numerous other Roman structures of religious or historical import, including the Pantheon, the Aqueduct, the Colosseum, the Rotunda of St. Stephen, and, on a nearby mountain, St. Benedict's Monte Casino Abbey and St. Scholastica of Subiaco, the location of the first Christian monastery.

Situated among the rocks and plants along the winding paved pathways of the grotto area beyond Jerusalem and Rome are dozens of other stand-alone structures. Some are memorials: an American flag made of concrete, colored marbles, and glass shards, dedicated to the students of St. Bernard College who were killed during World War II; an ornate tower in honor of the Red Cross workers who served during World War I. Some are smaller shrines: miniature grottos dedicated to St. Thérese of Lisieux, the Virgin Mary of Guadelupe, Our Lady of Fatima, the Agony in the Garden, and a replica of the famous pilgrimage site of the Lourdes shrine. Each shelters at least one small statue and is carefully decorated in the style of the Ave Maria Grotto.

Rome, Ave Maria Grotto

The vast majority of the other creations lining the paved walkways of this park are re-creations of famous buildings drawn from
sacred history, biblical mythology, and popular fantasy. Sacred sites
include Montserrat Abbey, a famous monastery and pilgrimage destination in Spain; the Bavarian Castle of Trausnitz and St. Martin's
Church, the tallest brick church in the world, located in Landshut,
Bavaria; the Benedictine monastery in Seoul, Korea; the World
Peace Church in Hiroshima, Japan; the Immaculate Conception
Cathedral in Mobile, Alabama (the first church in the United States
dedicated to the Virgin Mary); and the buildings of St. Bernard
Abbey itself.

Biblical scenes include a Noah's Ark perched high and dry on
a large flat stone, complete with little plastic animal pairs like the
ones I remember collecting with ARCO fill-ups on road trips as a

child. Nearby is the Tower of Babel, which the ancient postdiluvians built as a sign of unity, "lest we be scattered abroad upon the face of the whole earth," and which God destroyed lest they become too godlike in the process, scattering them and their tongues just as they had feared. Around the tower's base are little signs naming it in several different languages. The top of the tower is missing, knocked off by the hand of a worried God.

Other structures from ancient Near Eastern mythology include the Hanging Gardens of Babylon, one of the Seven Wonders of the World, here presented as a complex of garden terraces above a four-foot-wide pool. Toy elephants are thoughtfully placed among its flowers and columns. Its walls are covered with purple, yellow, and aqua tiles, making it stand out exotically from the nearby earth-toned Ark and tower, perhaps signaling its extrabiblical status.

Like the Tower and Ark, the Hanging Gardens exhibit is an imaginary reconstruction from the realm of mythology. But the most fanciful reconstruction of all the mythic spaces in Ave Maria Grotto is the Temple of the Fairies, a complex of colorful buildings, towers, and spires elaborately decorated with rows of shells, tiles, pebbles, marbles, crystals, lava rocks, precious stones, old cold-cream jars, and shiny columns that appear to be made from empty lipstick tubes. In the temple's front yard there are small statues and concrete trees resembling menorahs with shells at the ends of their branches. To the right of the temple is a mountain made of piled rocks from which sprout colorfully striped columns, like candy-canes. At the top of each is a piece of broken glass embedded in a blop of concrete. On the other side of the mountain, and connected to the temple by a winding trail, is a simple hamlet with two windows and a red roof. A nearby sign reads HANSEL AND GRETEL VISIT THE TEMPLE OF THE FAIRIES.

Fairylands have their underbellies, and this one is no exception.

In a damp and shady cavern underneath the temple, a winged dragon with a ridge of tiny white stones running down its spine stretches toward the light, its pounded sheet metal tongue sticking out from a gaping, craggy mouth, its glassy red marble eyes gazing hungrily at the path above, apparently watching for the children to arrive.

Interspersed throughout the area are various creations masquerading as plants: a cluster of pastel dessert plates blossoming from a flower pot perched atop a concrete trunk covered with seashells; starfish-like flowers, or flower-like starfishes, embedded with red marbles and plastic beads, sprouting on bent stalks of rusty rebar from deep green patches of fern and ivy. Just as the many miniature buildings seem simultaneously realistic and fantastical, these plant-like creations seem simultaneously to imitate and mock nature in a single whimsical gesture.

Ave Maria Grotto attracts an average of forty thousand visitors each year. On a weekend day during peak season, which runs from Easter Sunday through early October, the grotto hosts two hundred or more. Many come in groups from local churches, Catholic as well as Protestant. Others come as tourists from other parts of the country and world. Attracted by the many replicas of famous buildings, teachers from local elementary schools take their classes there on field trips in the spring and early fall.

My family visited Ave Maria Grotto on a sunny weekday in June—the day after we visited Cross Garden, in fact. By noon there were more than a hundred people roaming the pathways that wind among the rocks, trees, buildings, and shrines of the grotto area. At least half were children between the ages of five and fifteen. Traveling in packs, they showed at least as much excited fascination with the various creations as the adults did prayerful reverence. Enchanted by the strange mix of otherworldly fancy and earnest recreation, everyone expressed amazement, sometimes in sighs too deep for words, at the remarkable craftsmanship, imagination, and love invested in the various works. Indeed, what holds all the works together, what gives them soul, is a feeling that every little creation has been endowed with loving devotion by its maker. Which begs the question, who is its maker?

Brother Joseph

Ave Maria Grotto is indeed a labor of love, the love of a lay brother named Joseph Zoettl. Brother Joseph died in 1962. By all accounts a very shy and unpretentious man, his story might have gone untold but for a friend, Dr. John Morris, who worked with others close to him to write an outstanding biography, *Miniature Miracle: A Biography of Brother Joseph Zoettl, O.S.B.*

Brother Joseph was born Michael Zoettl in 1878 in the predominantly Catholic town of Landshut, Bavaria, north of Munich. A small boy of weak constitution, Michael was often sick and suffered from heart palpitations. He was not a particularly outstanding student, but did relatively well in his religion courses, so his stepmother decided he would become a priest. In 1892, his family met a Benedictine father who was recruiting a group of religious potentials to go with him to the new monastery of St. Bernard in the young German-American town of Cullman, Alabama. The recruiter was reluctant to take Michael on account of his physical frailties, but the Zoettl family eventually convinced him to do so. In January of 1892, at the age of thirteen, Michael set sail with his new religious comrades on the *Suavia* for the United States, never to return to his homeland and family.

Michael immediately fell in love with his new home in Cullman, where he and his colleagues built the new monastery while carrying out their studies. As a student, he excelled in conduct, politeness, and punctuality, if not academics. His abbot didn't recommend him for the priesthood, but did invite him to stay on at St. Bernard as a lay brother. Preferring work with his hands over book studies anyway, he gladly accepted. It was during his novitiate that he was given the additional name of Brother Joseph.

During his early years as a lay brother, Joseph worked in the dining hall and kitchen on campus and as a housekeeper for priests in nearby towns. In 1911 he was assigned to operate the powerhouse, shoveling coal and maintaining its boilers and generator. Despite his small stature (under five feet tall, under a hundred pounds) and chronic back troubles, he did the job well and it remained his primary occupation throughout the rest of his working life at the monastery.

In what little free time he had, Brother Joseph began creating things from throwaways—picture frames for altar spaces, small grottos made from slag, motors powered by falling sand. In 1918 he started making miniature replicas of buildings from concrete. Near the monastery's outdoor recreation area he built a small church and a collection of other buildings that came to be known as "Little Jerusalem." This work began to attract visitors, who distracted the brothers from their work and devotional life, and so Joseph was ordered not to create any more installations on the premises. This prohibition lasted for several years. But his creative energy found other outlets, as he made thousands and thousands of small grottos, tiny replicas of caves formed from concrete and decorated with glass and other ornaments. The abbey sold them for fifteen to twenty-five cents a piece. Many of them can still be found in local living rooms and on local lawns. To this day no one knows how many he made altogether, but word has it that he stopped counting at five thousand.

Recognizing Brother Joseph's remarkable gifts, his abbot commissioned him in 1932 to create a full-size grotto on the St. Bernard campus, but in another location that would not interrupt the monastic disciplines of the brothers. The hillside area that had served as the quarry during the building phase of the monastery was selected, and Brother Joseph began work. Not that he was allowed to quit his day job at the powerhouse. He set up a shop in a room next to the furnace so he could work on the grotto and other creations without neglecting his other duties.

Joseph built the reinforced concrete shell in his shop, one section at a time. With the help of other brothers, he moved each section over to the quarry area and installed it. Rebar and railroad ties were planted in the ceiling to serve as reinforcements for the stalactites. The crushed marble that lines the mouth and interior of the grotto came by (providential?) accident: a train carrying a freight car full of marble crashed on the nearby L&N railroad, and the owner of the shipment donated the smashed remains to the monastery. The hand-carved Carrara marble statues of Our Mother of Prompt Succor, St. Benedict, and St. Scholastica, each weighing about a ton, were imported from Italy and carefully placed in the grotto once everything else was complete. On Ascension Day 1934, the Ave Maria Grotto was consecrated. The first creation and centerpiece of the grotto area, the brothers still consider it to be Brother Joseph's masterwork.

Over the next three decades, Brother Joseph surrounded the grotto with numerous other miniature replicas of sacred cities, shrines, and other structures drawn from Christian history, biblical narrative, myth, and legend. First, in the same year the grotto was completed, he used a wheelbarrow to relocate the buildings of his "Little Jerusalem" to the quarry area from their place near the brothers' recreation area behind the monastery. Years later he created a second Jerusalem situated within a larger biblical story-world context of Scenes from the Holy Land (the "Little Jerusalem" now sits to the far right of the Scenes exhibit). Then came Rome. And the rest is history. He completed his last work, a replica of the famous grotto shrine at Lourdes, France, in 1958, at age eighty, only three years before his death.

Prayers in Stone

Besides concrete, Brother Joseph's building materials consisted primarily of various ornamental objects, cultural or natural, that had no value to anyone else: lipstick tubes, cold-cream jars, broken plates and glass, plastic beads, marbles, bent forks and spoons, rebar, lava rocks, crushed marble, pebbles, seashells. He made the two domes on the Immaculate Conception Cathedral of Mobile, Alabama, from toilet bowl floats. For St. Peter's Basilica in Rome, he formed the tiny pillars that line the walkway around the courtyard by pouring concrete into broken test-tubes from the abbey school's lab and then breaking the glass once the concrete had dried. He made the large central dome of the church from a birdcage.

With growing numbers of visitors to the grotto came a growing number of friends and admirers who sent Brother Joseph pieces of jewelry, small statues, and other ornamental objects in hopes he might be able to use them in his creations. He expressed his own gratitude to these many patrons with the Tower of Thanks, one of his more exuberantly whimsical works. Elaborately decorated with various kinds of seashells, tiny colored tiles, broken plates, and large leaves molded from concrete, it is topped with three glass fishing balls from Ireland that look like eyeballs sprouting from the ends of branches.

Except for the abbey and the two buildings from his childhood home of Landshut (which he last saw at age thirteen), Brother

Joseph never visited the buildings he re-created. His replicas are based entirely on photographs and drawings he found on postcards and in books. His tools, too, were simple: a couple of spoons, a kitchen knife, files, hole punches, trowels, and brushes. Refusing squares or levels, he "eyeballed" every building's placement, dimensions, angles, and proportions.

Monroe Sears, a tall, sturdy, elderly man with an understated air, has worked full-time at the abbey since 1956, keeping the grounds and maintaining the plant among many other duties. Mr. Sears worked closely with Brother Joseph as his assistant for about five years toward the end of his life. Brother Joe, as he is affectionately remembered, had never been very strong. He was a chronic pipe smoker, and during his last years his breathing became very weak. Mr. Sears would watch him from a distance as he wandered among his creations, pulling a weed here or there. Sometimes he would become too tired to get himself down from the exhibits on his own, and Mr. Sears would carry him in his arms and set him on a nearby bench.

Mr. Sears's admiring stories paint a picture of a very humble and shy man who preferred to remain hidden in the background of his ever more famous creations. When visitors happened to see him working on the exhibits, he was perfectly willing to pass as an assistant or gardener.

It seems that his primary form of expression to others was through his creations—"sermons in stone," as Mr. Sears and some of the brothers call them. But they're more than sermons, certainly. Their kerygma, their meaning, their voice, is not really a sermonic message but something much more visual if also more richly ambiguous and otherworldly: a quite concrete embodiment of his religious vision of the world, which was a world of sacred narrative populated with loci of profound devotional meaning and miracle. Ave Maria

Grotto is a microcosm of Brother Joseph's mind, a topography of his religious imagination.

More than any form of *public* expression, however, these works are deeply personal "prayers in stone." Indeed, despite the tremendous popularity of Ave Maria Grotto, which has become something of a pilgrimage destination in its own right, I came to see these works as the public remains of Brother Joseph's very concrete and very personal, inward-looking form of devotional practice. His process of creative work was his means of meditating on the sacred places and sacred narratives of his faith, of embodying them and making them his own. These works are Brother Joseph's own creative and imaginative pilgrimages to places he would never be able to visit otherwise.

Some might presume that the tremendous, sometimes awe-inspiring attention Brother Joseph gave to every little detail of every work reflects his desire to "get it right," to accurately represent the historical landmarks or story worlds he was re-creating. Perhaps there is some truth to this, but it doesn't explain the fantastically whimsical ornamentation that so pervades everything here. No, I believe that the great care and artistic flare given to each little creation in this place testifies to the importance of his own creative *process* as a form of religious meditation. For the work of art is never simply an expression of the artist's imagination. Rather, the process of creating actually shapes that imagination. For Brother Joseph, the meticulous process of creating both expressed and shaped his religious imagination. As he populated this hillside of the monastery's old quarry, he was populating his own mind.

Note, moreover, that in Brother Joseph's religious imaginary, Bible lands and fairylands are part of the same sacred world. The Temple of the Fairies is a stone's roll away from the Temple of Jerusalem. Hansel and Gretel live very near Martha and Mary. They're neighbors. Brother Joseph's religious imaginary, his garden of revelation, is a world in which multiple stories—some history, some myth, some fantasy—occupy the same sacred space. It is clear, moreover, that he devoted just as much painstaking care and creative ingenuity to the fairylands as he did to historical landmarks and biblical holy lands. He treated them as no less sacred spaces than the others.

Near the top of the hillside in the grotto area, Brother Joseph made a shrine dedicated to the Benedictine monastic order. Its centerpiece is a tall column covered in large seashells and topped with a circular cross in which the Latin word PAX ("peace") is written in marbles. Behind this column is a sunburst, also in shell-covered concrete, with two smaller towers on either side. At the base of each of these two smaller towers is a word: ORA on the left, LABORA on the right, written in pieces of black stone. *Ora et labora*, "pray and work," the mantra of the Benedictines. Appropriate words for a shrine dedicated to Brother Joseph's monastic order, certainly, they speak even more profoundly to his own specific lifework in Ave Maria Grotto. This was both his labora and his ora, indeed a perfect marriage of the two.

The great paradox is that Brother Joseph's very deeply personal ora et labora in the garden has resulted in a very popular public religious attraction, drawing tens of thousands of people every year. This would be no surprise to Brother Joseph. His work drew public attention from the get-go, beginning with his first "Little Jerusalem." For him, however, what seemed to matter most was that he be allowed to continue creating.

Since his death, one sees a certain grassroots canonization of Brother Joseph in progress. Not that he is on the radar of the Vatican or anything official like that (then again, maybe he is). But an increasingly reverential popular interest in the life behind this lifework has grown. Responding to this interest, the abbey's brochures and tour guide for the grotto focus at least as much on Brother Joseph and his life story as they do on the works themselves. Dr. Morris's biography of Brother Joseph, *Miniature Miracle*, a book written with much love and admiration for a friend, reads very like a hagiography, a sacred biography. Indeed, the title highlights a theme that runs throughout the book, namely that Brother Joseph's life and lifework, taken as a whole, constitutes something of a miracle.

Most fascinating to me in this regard was a glass display case in the abbey bookstore (also the ticket counter and entrance to the grotto) with a small handwritten card reading "the tools used by Brother Joseph." Neatly arranged on a blue blanket inside are several dozen small items: a pair of thick-rimmed glasses, two pipes with tape wrapped around well-chewed mouthpieces, pencils, a couple spoons, a kitchen knife, and several simple tools, all caked with white mortar as though cleaning them would have removed some of Brother Joseph's creative life force that still adheres to them. Reverently displayed, untouchable behind the glass, these items have been set apart as sacred objects, the tools of mediation between the creations outside and the hand of the creator.

Filled with admiration for his friend, Mr. Sears gave me a private tour of Brother Joseph's workshop, two small rooms in the basement of the old powerhouse building. Along the cinder block walls of the larger room, which he used for storage, are bookshelves holding dozens of cigar boxes, plastic trays, and cutout milk jugs filled with different kinds of ornaments—jewelry pieces, seashells, beads, glass fragments, tiles, and other shiny bits that Brother Joseph had acquired over the years. Mr. Sears explained that another local artist is now using these to repair and refurbish older works that have been sitting in local house gardens and on lawns for decades.

Next to this storage area is a smaller room, about the size of a water closet. On one wall is a gray slate tabletop—half of a retired pool table—resting on a base of barrels and cinder blocks. This, Mr. Sears told me, was where Brother Joseph did all his work. Unlike the tools displayed in the bookstore, however, this space has not been set apart as sacred in any obvious way. It is now being used by those who maintain the plant and grounds. When I saw it, the table was covered with wrenches, work gloves, gas cans, PVC joints, stretches of garden hose, and bug spray.

The reverence with which Mr. Sears revealed this locus of the Brother's creative work to me stood in some tension with the mundane, workaday appearance of the table itself. I must admit that I felt a desire to set it apart too, to protect the sanctity of this altar space against the desecrating encroachment of profane workaday activities.

Yet I have a feeling that Brother Joseph would prefer it this way. He might even remind me that ora et labora is the work of all in the community, that the labora of fixing leaks and repairing small motors is as much an ora as is Evensong in the chapel, that the whole mess and noise that happens here every day is an oratorio of praise to the creator of all.

Chapter Ten

FOLK ART CHURCH

Paradise Gardens
Summerville, Georgia

PARADISE GARDEN: GARDEN OF POWER—GARDEN OF LI-
GHT—GARDEN OF THE BIBLE—GARDEN OF INVENTIONS—
HOWARD FINSTER WAS INSPIRED OF GOD TO BUILD THIS
GARDEN—THIS GARDEN HAS ABOUT 30 YEARS WORK IN
IT—THIS GARDEN IS FREE TO YOU—GARDEN OF FRUIT—
GARDEN OF FLOWERS—GARDEN OF BIRDS AND WILD-
LIFE—GARDEN OF SCULPTURE—GARDEN OF LOVE—GARDEN
OF ART—GARDEN OF STRUCTURES—GARDEN OF WALKS—GAR-
DEN OF FELLOWSHIP—GARDEN OF SERMONS.

> —*Howard Finster, Paradise Gardens,*
> *hand-painted sign above carport*

As we traveled south in our motor home along Georgia State Highway 27 through the towns of Chicamauga and Lafayette, we passed
miles of Civil War battle grounds, wide grassy fields studded with
cannons and memorial markers where thousands of soldiers were
mowed down by fellow Americans. Pacific Northwesterners by birth
and by choice, it wasn't until Clover and I moved to Atlanta for
graduate school that we began to fathom the complexity of southern
cultural memory concerning that war. While no northerner can

speak for such aspects of the southern experience, there is no question that these and other battlefields are highly ambiguous sacred landmarks, holy scars that haunt the southern landscape with memories not only of heroism and cultural pride but also defeat, loss, and shame.

A little farther north on Highway 27, just outside Summerville in a modest neighborhood behind the Sav A Ton gas station and kitty corner from Hayes Correctional Institute, a state prison, there is a very different sort of southern memorial, one that offers a very different window onto southern culture: Howard Finster's Paradise Gardens, a testimony to the religious imagination, a place of artistic creation and creative community.

In the Beginning

In 1976, itinerant preacher and sometime handyman Howard Finster was rubbing paint on a bicycle in his garden. In the paint on his finger he saw a face. "Paint sacred art," it told him. Sixty years old at the time, he replied that he didn't think he could do art because he wasn't a professional. "I don't have no education in that." The voice kept asking him, "How do you know?" Eventually he pulled a dollar bill from his wallet, tacked it onto a piece of plywood, and began painting a portrait of George Washington. So began his folk art ministry at what soon came to be called Paradise Gardens, a neighborhood block of religious visionary works by Finster and other artists. This wasn't the first divine vision he'd ever been given. According to his daughter, Beverly, he had his first vision at the age of three: standing in the fields of Alabama, near the home where he was born, he saw his deceased sister, Abby, come down from the heavens on a stairway of clouds. He felt called to preach at the age of sixteen and

soon had his own tent in which he hosted revival meetings throughout Alabama, Georgia, and Tennessee. A successful preacher who
often illustrated his Bible teachings with drawings, Rev. Finster
served as pastor of a number of churches, including a fifteen-year
stint at Chelsea Baptist Church close to Menlo, Georgia. But he quit
preaching when, one Sunday evening, he asked people what he had
preached on Sunday morning and no one could remember. Eventually the face on the finger showed him another way to preach, and he
continued creating sacred art in this "garden of sermons," as the sign
above a carport describes it, for the rest of his life.

I first heard about Howard Finster in the mid-1980s, when he did
album-cover art for R.E.M.'s *Reckoning* (the song titles are written
on purple and green intestine-like tubes, snaking through a black
background etched with faces) and Talking Heads' *Little Creatures* (a
brightly colored world of wedding cake castles and black mountains
under a sky populated by smiling cloud puffs, with lead singer David
Byrne in tight whites carrying a globe on his shoulders). By that time
Rev. Finster was gaining some national attention through his associations with the growing southern counterculture centered in the
university town of Athens, Georgia. Many younger alternative
music enthusiasts like me first learned about him when he was featured in the documentary film *Athens, Georgia Inside/Out*, which
celebrated the raw, experimental, and distinctly southern sounds
of bands like R.E.M., The B-52s, and Pylon in and around Athens.
While attending graduate school in the Atlanta area in the late
1980s, Clover and I knew several student colleagues who made
trips to Paradise Gardens, returning with portraits of Elvis and Finster's Cadillac painted on pieces of cutout plywood, covered front
and back with autobiographical statements and biblical messages.
Sadly, we never made it out there during that time. More than a

decade later, a visit to Paradise Gardens was a must for our first summer trip in search of roadside religion. Indeed, I'd say that it was the one place on our itinerary that really was, for me, a pilgrimage destination.

Of course, it was bound to be different from what it had been in the late 1980s. Since then Rev. Finster's art had become world famous. His works were featured in major folk art shows and permanent exhibits in nearly every major museum in the United States and many others throughout the world. He had appeared on numerous television shows, including Johnny Carson and *Good Morning America*. And his art was fetching high prices in galleries from San Francisco to Paris. Then, in October 2001, less than a year before we visited, Howard Finster died of complications related to diabetes.

But I did experience my own sort of revelation while at Paradise Gardens, and I don't know if I would have gotten it back in grad school. Here it is: Paradise Gardens is not about Rev. Finster. Despite the expectations of visitors who come from all over the world in hopes of having a more direct experience of this man of vision, in a very profound sense Paradise Gardens is not about him. It is about the work of a community, a religious community in some sense, but also an artistic community. Paradise Gardens is a church, and Rev. Finster was its founding pastor. And the calling of this church is to create.

Work in Progress

Passing through the narrow chain-link gate next to the small Finster home, one enters immediately into another world, an Edenic jungle of paintings, sculptures, and buildings nestled among trees and muddy trails, overgrown with weeds and vines. Much of the artwork is rusting, cracking, and peeling from decades of exposure to the elements. Yet the general feeling pervading the place is one of generativity, creative energy, life.

Two large structures provide a degree of orientation within the space of the Gardens. One is the famous Garden Chapel, a three-tier round tower topped with a spire that reaches about fifty feet into the air. It looks something like a cross between a leaning wedding cake and the Tower of Babel. Each of its circular levels is decorated with carefully jigsawed wood trim and rows of small windows framed with shiny metal. Although not located physically in the center of the space, it nonetheless functions as the orienting point for the entire Garden. It is the temple, the axis mundi of this paradisal universe. According to signs nearby, the Garden Chapel has hosted thousands of free weddings and school groups. When I visited, however, it was closed to visitors, as it was in need of substantial structural repairs to keep it from toppling over.

The second major structure providing orientation in the Gardens is a long, covered walkway cutting more or less diagonally across the property. Built in the early 1990s, its floor is about nine feet off the ground, set on wooden posts like a beachfront pier running off into the woods. At regular intervals, holes shaped like arched church windows have been cut into the exterior walls. Underneath the walkway there are glass window boxes in which apparently random collections of art and other found stuff are displayed or stored. The story is that Rev. Finster wanted to collect everything in the world, so that his paradise would contain all of creation, natural and cultural alike. Paradise Gardens was to be his own cabinet of curiosities.

Inside the walkway itself are numerous works of art, some by Rev. Finster but most by friends. Here as elsewhere, his own work is mixed in with the work of others. It was already becoming clear that

Garden Chapel, Paradise Gardens

anyone interested only in Rev. Finster's individual artworks would quickly grow frustrated in Paradise Gardens. It is a community effort, indeed an expression of community, a place of creation for many, perhaps for any. If I had drawn something and pinned it to the wall, it would probably be there today. Rev. Finster called himself "the World's Minister of the Folk Art Church." Clearly, the theology of this church embraces an ecclesiology firmly grounded on belief in "the priesthood of all believers."

In addition to these two very prominent structures and the Finster home, there are several other buildings. Connected to the back side of the Folk Art Church is a shotgun-shack style house that stretches to the back corner of the lot. On the exterior wall facing Rena Avenue there are large murals of bright-eyed people with big smiles. On another wall is a portrait of George Washington, and around the corner from George is a painting of the Second Coming of Christ, surrounded by clouds with smiling faces which Rev. Finster called "resting souls."

Elsewhere in the woodsy parts of the property are miniature chapels, decorated inside and out with all imaginable varieties of dangling things. Near the Finster home sits a larger red and white chapel with arched window cutouts that match the ones on the walkway. Fitted with a dozen or so rows of old wooden church pews, it could cozily seat close to a hundred. Between the arched openings on its exterior walls are small wooden boards on which various scriptural passages are written. Blue and yellow plastic tubes, strung together like deli wieners, dangle from the edges of the roof.

Near this larger chapel, an old white Cadillac is parked under a carport's sagging roof. The date on the license plate is 1976—the same year in which the finger talked to Rev. Finster. All over the surfaces of the car, pictures and written words explain its significance. Next to a portrait of a man in a blue suit with long black hair is the caption, VICTOR VACCINTO DONATED THIS CADILLAC TO HOWARD. VICTOR IS DIRECTOR OF ART AT UNIVERSITY OF WAKE FOREST IN NORTH CAROLINA. Next to Victor is a portrait of Jesus wearing a crown and holding a softball-size globe in his hand. Next to Jesus is a portrait of Rev. Finster himself with the accompanying words: BY

HOWARD FINSTER WORLDS MINISTER OF FOLK ART CHURCH. MAN OF VISIONS FROM THREE YEARS OLD. 2000 AND 63 PAINTINGS SINCE 1976. All over the rear trunk are portraits, some clearly resembling famous political leaders and celebrities, most without identification. Words painted across the narrow section of metal above the rear window serve as a title for the whole scene: THE DEAD AND LIVING ONE TOGETHER.

Every building, every object, every surface is a canvas for art. And each creation becomes something to make more art on, so that every work becomes a layer in an ongoing accrual of creative generation. What one sees on the surface is simply the most recent creative visitation (maybe yesterday, maybe twenty years ago) by...who knows? With few exceptions (for example, the Caddy bearing Finster's signature), the works here are not identified with their creators. The place is both archive and work in progress.

Next to one pathway, surrounded by empty cans, ceramic jars, and other junk, is a gigantic white clown shoe, like the ones Ronald McDonald wears. It's about three feet tall and six feet long, and a verse from Paul's letter to the Romans is written across the toes: "How beautiful are the feet of those who spread the gospel of peace." Not the most beautiful shoe one could make to illustrate this passage. Most of us probably imagine something more like Hermes' winged foot as it appears in FTD flower delivery ads. But the juxtaposition of a big clunky old-fashioned boot and words describing beautiful feet spreading the Gospel of peace is jarring, ultimately calling attention to the text itself, opening it for reflection in fresh ways.

Throughout Paradise Gardens, nailed to walls, leaning against trees and rocks, are painted boards. Some are jigsawed shapes painted to resemble angels and secular saints, such as a badly faded bust of Henry Ford nailed to the outside of the raised walkway, on which is written, among other things, HENRY FORD. INVENTED. THE HORSELESS-CHARIOT — DESCRIBED BY THE PROPHET AND PUT THE WORLD ON MOTOR WHEELS, a reference to Ezekiel's vision of the cherubim. Ironically, Ford has become a vehicle for scripture.

In fact, most of the painted boards found everywhere in Paradise Gardens contain nothing but words from the Bible, primarily Psalms and sayings of Jesus. Many are no longer readable, their plywood layers separating and their text fading from decades of exposure to Georgia downpours and heat waves. It's easy to imagine the street preacher Rev. Finster transcribing these verses from memory, peopled as his imagination was with biblical literature. For him, I imagine, such transcriptions, done throughout his lifework in Paradise Gardens, may have provided a means of meditating on scripture. For visitors, these scripture boards give new meaning to Rev. Finster's description of the place as a "garden of the Bible ... a garden of sermons." Indeed, they make Paradise Gardens into its own special kind of "land of the Bible."

Ministry of Love

In some respects there is a kinship between this place and another garden we've visited: Bill Rice's Cross Garden, which was begun only a year after Paradise Gardens (1977). Both are widely acknowledged as works of outsider art, although Paradise Gardens has certainly enjoyed far more appreciation among "insider" aficionados of outsider art. Both places combine buildings (chapels, etc.) and found objects, and both use nearly every surface as a canvas for words, often words of judgment and hellfire. Indeed, Finster, like Rice, saw himself as a modern-day Noah—a "second Noah," as he put it in some of his sermons, sent from another planet to tell people to get ready. "They laughed at me, just like they laughed at Noah

"How beautiful are the feet," Paradise Gardens

when he was building the Ark." Indeed, like Rice, Finster saw his art primarily as a means of preaching that judgment is coming, that hell is real, and that we all had better be ready. Scrawled on the back of a little jigsawed angel I have from Paradise Gardens, for example, it is written, JESUS IS COMING BACK. PSALM 34:7 THE ANGEL OF THE LORD EMCAMPETH ROUND ABOUT THEM THAT FEAR HIM, AND DELIVERETH THEM. BE READY.

Linda, who works at the art shop and sells tickets to Paradise Gardens, was a close friend of Rev. Finster, whom she called Pa. "Pa would do that all the time," she told me as I read the back of my angel for the first time. "He'd put scriptures and Bible messages on the fronts and backs of his art. He knew people liked his art and he used it to get his word out."

My family spent the evening in a little cottage on the property, just behind the garage. The main bedroom was decorated with paintings by Rev. Finster and other artists. The theme was the Garden of Eden—not the uplifting, paradisiacal garden variety, but the original-sin and serpent kind. One painting was particularly striking. Best viewed while lying on the bed propped up by pillows, it was a cutout depicting the DEVIL AND HIS WIFE. In the foreground the Devil and another female figure (Eve?), naked but for red and blue striped shorts, caress one another while a serpent bites or licks the female figure on the behind. In the background, a fourth figure called CHILD OF DEVIL watches on. Beneath the two figures is a text message warning against the evils of adultery:

IF YOU DEFILE YOUR BODY GOD WILL DESTROY STAY CLEAN! DON'T DEFILE YOUR BODY ADULTERY IS SEX WITHOUT MARRIAGE LEGAL SEX EVER WOMAN, HAS HER OWN HUSBAND, EVERR MAN, HAS HIS OWN WIFE. THIS IS LEGAL MARRIAGE. SEX IT CAN STILL BE NASTY AND HARMFUL. SO MANY DEASES NOW YOU CAN CATCH SO EASY TO GET DEFILED. WATCH.

Not exactly the sort of message young artists and R.E.M. fans are generally looking to hear. But what drew them to Rev. Finster and his Paradise Gardens was something else, something visible between nearly every line of text (okay, not in the text on STDs I just quoted) and in the peaceful, smiling faces of every celebrity, friend, and "resting soul" watching visitors from the painted boards and walls of Paradise Gardens: a genuine love of all people. A pickup truck camper sitting on jacks in the middle of the Gardens says it all. Painted across the top, in large block letters, is the warning, TIME WAITS FOR NO ONE. BE READY WHEN GOD CALLS. TAKE TIME TO BE HOLY, and then across the bottom is another message, frequently repeated in Rev. Finster's paintings: I NEVER SEEN A PERSON I DIDNT LOVE.

Those who knew him best readily attest to the truth of this declaration. "He loved everybody," Linda told me, "and those kids who'd come listen to him all the time, they knew it." Even after he and his wife, Paula, moved to another house in 1996, he would come to Paradise Gardens every Sunday to talk with guests. "He'd sit in that chair there," she said, pointing to a well-worn black leather armchair now prominently displayed in the center of the main room of the house. "He'd sit in that chair out on the porch and play his banjo and sing gospel songs and preach. Sometimes he'd preach about the evils of drugs and judgment and that sort of thing. Maybe not all the kids there agreed with him on that stuff. A lot of 'em weren't saved or anything. But he loved 'em and they knew it, so they'd listen anyway." Hellfire though there may be, Paradise Gardens was and is clearly a place of loving hospitality, and its host was also pa and pastor to all who entered its gates.

Created in the Image

As Rev. Finster's fame grew in the 1990s, he found himself devoting more and more time to special exhibitions and speaking and teaching engagements as well as producing artwork for sale. As a result he had less time to tend his own garden. Many of his early creations have gone so many seasons untended that they have become part of their natural surroundings. It's easy to miss them altogether while wandering through the Gardens. In an open grassy space near the raised walkway, for example, there's a round leafy green mound about twenty feet high and thirty feet wide. On first glance it looks like an enormous bush. But look a little more closely and you'll see a rust brown mass of bicycle frames, lawn-mower push handles, and other tubular metal artifacts welded together into a giant sculpture.

Yet even as some of its pieces are overtaken by weeds or biodegraded into the soil, the Gardens themselves felt very much alive. I sensed a sweet, sweet spirit in this place, a spirit of generosity and hospitality. It is open, unfinished, in process. A space of invention, it invites participation. THIS GARDEN IS FREE TO YOU—GARDEN OF FRUIT—GARDEN OF FLOWERS—GARDEN OF BIRDS AND WILDLIFE—GARDEN OF SCULPTURE—GARDEN OF LOVE—GARDEN OF ART—GARDEN OF STRUCTURES—GARDEN OF WALKS—GARDEN OF FELLOW-SHIP. . . . Although I was alone in the Gardens, I did feel like it was a communal space, a space of fellowship in celebration of human creativity as sacred art. If this garden succeeds in creating a sacred space for visitors, it does so not by the genius of Finster's individual pieces of visionary art and architecture. It's not his individual presence that one feels there, but rather the collective fellowship of those he invited there to participate in its creation, the fellowship of the Folk Art Church, which he served as minister. At the theological and experiential center of this church and its garden is human creativity. What makes this place sacred is that it's a place of creation.

It took a revelation, a word of the Lord of the Folk Art Church, if you will, for me really to get it. Like most visitors, I had come to the Gardens in search of the creative genius of Rev. Finster, and expected to find it in seeing and touching the material objects he had created there. I was initially frustrated with, let's say, the lack of clear authorship and proper referencing of sources.

I had left the family back in the apartment and had been wandering, half-dazed from the profusion of created things, for an hour or so. The sun had dropped behind the trees, and it was growing dark. I found myself slightly lost and disoriented in a jungley back corner of the property. The little narrow muddy trail I was on seemed almost like an alternative entrance to the Gardens. Finger-painted on the back of a round rusty metal sign whose front side faced in the direction of the main entrance were the words, WELCOME TO PARADISE GARDENS. GOD IS LOVE.

To the right of the sign was a small building, which I believe had once been Finster's bicycle repair shop. Vines were growing up the outside walls and in and out of broken window panes. Its tin roof was brown with rust and covered with clumps of pine needles and cones. As though imitating the forces of nature that were gradually overtaking it, someone had painted green vine-like curly lines all over its weathered white siding. Large glass balls were hanging by wires from the overhang of the roof, and cans and bottles adorned the windows and walls. The effect was that the cultural artifacts, removed from their utilitarian contexts and made entirely ornamental, had become one with nature's vines and rust and needles. Like other older works in Paradise Gardens, the building had become part of the Gardens' ecology, emerging from and crumbling into the soil.

On the wall just below the windowsill near an old toilet tank, I noticed a message, written in wooden buttons nailed to the siding. GOD CREATES, it said. A simple enough statement of faith, and one not unrelated to the whole Paradise theme. But as I pondered it, I began to see a deeper meaning. This written statement that God creates is, after all, a creation in its own right. As is the building on which it's written. As is the whole "garden of fellowship" known as Paradise Gardens.

In biblical tradition, Paradise or the Garden of Eden is the jewel of God's original creation. It is the first human home, where God created them, male and female, in God's own image. In the first chapter of Genesis, we read that on the sixth day, as the culmination of the entire work of creation, God created human beings in God's own image. But what does it mean to say that humans were created

"GOD CREATES," Paradise Gardens

in the image of God? Many things to many people, no doubt, but what we know by that point in Genesis 1 is that God is, above all, creative in life-giving and world-making ways. In this light, to be creative, to create, *is* to be in the image of God. To be in the image of God is to be creative like the creator. Creativity itself is the image of God. The human form divine, as William Blake put it. Imago dei: the *art act*.

Paradise Gardens is a place of redemption. Adam and Eve were banished from the garden, and God went with them. But here we have a return to the garden and a return of the garden as the place of communion with the divine. Creativity becomes a means of redemption and restoration. Paradise Gardens is a work of communal creation that proclaims itself, through that very work, to restore humanity to its divine image. It's a return to Genesis, a return to being "in the beginning."

It was not exactly a burning-bush experience, and I wasn't about to remove my shoes in the mud. But at that moment, staring at the buttons on the wall, I did feel as though I were standing on holy ground, addressed by another whose name I did not know. Here in this jungley, otherworldly yet strangely familiar place of creation, a handful of buttons spoke volumes to me. Here the very substance of faith is the work itself, which is the shared fruit of living creatively in community. It is the substance that remains of the act of faith, that is, the act of creating, which is being in the divine image.

Conclusion

This is not the book I thought I was writing. Writing is about participating in a process that exceeds one's conscious, bookish intentions. It's a process of becoming, of genesis, in which one is written as much as one writes. And so the book I intended to write *about* religion has become, as well and perhaps especially, a *religious* book. What began as an exploration of roadside religious attractions and the stories behind them has wound up being a far more personal story of my own ambivalent search for faith.

It's fair to say that, for the most part, the mainstream American religious imagination, especially the mainstream American Christian religious imagination, has more often than not been oblivious to its own natural environment. As Native American historian of religion Vine Deloria has been particularly incisive in showing us, Christianity since the Roman era has developed as a fundamentally ungrounded, landless religion, highly adaptable to new environmental contexts but by the same token alien to the lands it travels and colonizes. This in dramatic contrast to Native American religious traditions, which center on experiences that are grounded in particular, local lands. Rather than growing and adapting in relation to the lands its people colonized, American Christianity chose to import another mythical world—the world of the Bible—and to lay it over the land, re-creating it in the image of its own story world. Which is why there are so many Zions, Bethlehems, Sinais, Canaans, and so on throughout the United States today.

We may well see some of the places explored in this book as extreme examples of this Christian tendency to impose its sacred story world on the natural landscapes of America. Think especially of the

Holy Land Experience in Orlando, an overlay of a particular imaginary construction of the "land of the Bible" on a place that has already been so completely transformed by commercial buildings, landscaping, and highway construction that its indigenous ecology is nearly impossible to recognize. And think of Fields of the Wood, where biblical texts inscribed in massive concrete letters are laid on top of freshly mown hillsides in a region that was for centuries the richly wooded heartland of the Cherokee peoples. Such places are indeed foreign religious impositions, almost entirely oblivious of the landscapes and ecologies they have overtaken.

But others, especially those that are the work of individuals rather than larger Christian organizations and institutions, have developed in relation to their natural context in such a way that they have indeed gained a kind of local, organic, grounded quality. Think of Holy Land USA, where the land of the Bible sinks itself into the lush woods of the Blue Ridge Mountains of Virginia. And think of Paradise Gardens, where the cultural and the natural blend together into an organic whole of creative composition and decomposition. Although in some respects religious importations and impositions, in other respects such places are rooted in the land and grow from it. Although in some respects they instantiate Deloria's point about American Christianity, in other respects they are exceptions. The extent to which they are exceptional, I think, has a lot to do with the extent to which they are personal, marked by the particular, local experiences and visions of a particular person.

These are the kinds of places I've found most compelling. In these places I experienced a correlation between connectedness to the land, personal authenticity, and openness to others. The more the place was locally grounded, rooted in its particular natural environment, the more uniquely personal it was, and the more hospitable it was to others. Hospitality is always local.

We are used to thinking of faith in terms of *belief*. Faith is believing in something enough to live by it without being able to know for sure that that belief is trustworthy. A leap of faith is a leap from the edge of certainty, beyond where knowledge and reason can take me. It's about embracing something I can only hope is true, envisioning something I can't see.

But there is another dimension to faith, I've come to realize, one that has less to do with belief and more to do with relationship. I mean faith as a leap of hospitality, that is, an opening toward an unknown other. Faith as vulnerability, risking relationship. The other might be God or it might be another human being. Indeed, in Christian tradition as in many other religious traditions, opening oneself in relation to God leads to opening oneself in relation to others. Jesus, quoting Torah, said that the greatest commandment was to "Love God with all your heart mind and strength," and then continued with another Torah passage, which he said follows directly from the first: "Love your neighbor as yourself." (When asked, "Who's my neighbor," he answered with the story of the Good Samaritan, which basically says that your neighbor is the one you least want to be your neighbor.)

Faith is a leap of hospitality, an opening of oneself to the other. It finds expression in welcoming the other into one's space, one's home, but also into one's self, one's inner life, one's dreams and visions. This is the lesson I learned about faith from places like Holy Land USA and Paradise Gardens, and from people like Bill and Marzell Rice and Richard Greene. Even when the message was daunting, if not repulsive (YOU WILL DIE. HELL IS HOT HOT HOT.), the gesture of the place and its creator was often one of self-exposure, a welcoming of the unknown other into relationship by revealing very personal religious experiences in a very open and vulnerable way.

Conclusion

Cynicism hounds faith. It is faith's most dogged antagonist. That's easy to see when we're thinking of faith as *belief* in something or someone beyond sufficient evidence. When we look at this other face of faith, the face of open hospitality and vulnerable self-revelation, we see another face of cynicism as well. If faith is a form of genuine, self-exposing relationship to the other, then cynicism is a form of disconnection and alienation from the other. The antidote to cynicism is relationship, the offering and receiving of hospitality.

In the places that most compelled and moved me, it was this leap of hospitality that I found most disarming of my plans for witty and wry observation. That feeling hasn't diminished since my visits. Quite the contrary. It has created in me a sense of obligation. I've come away with an experience of relationship born of a gesture of open self-revelation. Hospitality, offered and received, creates a relationship that is irrevocable. That changes everything. In light of such hospitality, I feel a certain sense of accountability, to which this book has become a personal response, a writing of my own story in conversation with theirs. Self-revelation invites response in kind. Which is why this is not the book I thought I was writing. But it is the book I needed to write.

Acknowledgments

What a long strange trip it's been. And what an incredible gift to have shared it with my family. I'm above all and ever grateful to Clover, colleague, counselor, dear reader, Presbyterian shaman, love of my life, for making this project her own, and for pushing me to make it my own in a more meaningful, self-reflective way. I thank our kids, Seth and Sophie, for joining in with such thoughtful openness and readiness for adventure.

I'm grateful to the people about whom I've written—those who create such fascinatingly strange religious marvels and those who look after them. To the extent that they have shared their stories and their spaces with me openly and honestly, I feel a tremendous sense of accountability to them. I hope that I've written about them well, with understanding and sympathy.

As ever, I thank members of the Tel Quel Theory Lunch and Praxis Breakfast group, especially Tod Linafelt and Brent Plate, for countless conversations and encouragements from the beginning. I also thank the many other friends and colleagues at Case and elsewhere who have offered insight and suggestion along the way, especially David Gunn, Bill Deal, Ted Steinberg, Ed Gemerchak, Sally Wile, Jana Riess, Lynne and Jeffrey Ford, Susan Griffith, Deb Krause, Bill Perman, Kyle Keefer, Bill Germano, Vince Miller, Pam Conover, and Burke Long. Thanks as well to the students in my "Roadside Religion" class at the Cleveland Ecumenical Institute for Religious Studies. And I am grateful for the support of those who work with me in the Baker-Nord Center for the Humanities at Case, who readily forgave me when I missed their deadlines while racing to meet press deadlines.

Acknowledgments

My editor at Beacon, Amy Caldwell, is a true master, handl
everything from serial commas to story arcs with felicity and ge
uine interest. I'm especially grateful to her for encouraging me to e>
plore what, beyond curiosity, drove me to these places. Thanks als‹
to editorial assistant Jennifer Yoon for persistent patience in moving
me and this book forward.

I've benefited much from opportunities to share my work in
progress in a number of different venues. Among them: the Robert
S. Mason Lecture at Georgetown University, an interview with
April Baer on Cleveland's NPR station WCPN, and presentations
at local churches including St. Peter Cathedral, Forest Hill Church,
Trinity Cathedral, Fairmount Baptist Church, and the Church of
the Covenant.

I am indebted to numerous scholarly works, which appear between the lines throughout this book. Here I want to mention two
which, although discovered after I was well underway, have been
particularly influential: John Beardsley's insightful and eloquent
Gardens of Revelation: Environments by Visionary Artists (New York:
Abbeville Press, 1995), and Burke O. Long's truly monumental
Imagining the Holy Land: Maps, Models, and Fantasy Travels (Bloom-
ington: Indiana University Press, 2002).

I do a lot of my writing in diners, and happily acknowledge
my unpayable debt to those I've most frequented in Cleveland:
Bill's, Tommy's, Dottie's (R.I.P.), Eat at Joe's, Michael's, the Inn on
Coventry, Yours Truly, Chuck's, and Big Al's. They know what "over
medium" means, and they can make it so with ease.

Finally, I thank my parents, Gerri and Clay, for their integrity of
faith, their interest in my work, and their belief in me. I dedicate this
book to the memory of my dad, whose life and death trace their way
through these pages in ways that continue to astonish me.